Business Networks in Japan

658.575 LAA

Hertfordshire
COUNTY COUNCIL
Community Information

been
exist
that
owth

usto-
argest
Cor-
have
rs in
ilized
study
inter-
hting
lizing

keting
He is

Routledge Advances in Asia-Pacific Business

Business Networks in Japan

Supplier–customer interaction in product development

Jens Laage-Hellman

London and New York

First published 1997
by Routledge
11 New Fetter Lane, London EC4P 4EE

Simultaneously published in the USA and Canada
by Routledge
29 West 35th Street, New York, NY 10001

Typeset in Times by Pure Tech India Limited, Pondicherry
Printed and bound in Great Britain by Redwood Books,
Trowbridge, Wiltshire

British Library Cataloguing in Publication Data

A catalogue record for this book is available from the British
Library

Library of Congress Cataloging in Publication Data
Laage-Hellman, Jens.
    Business networks in Japan: supplier–customer
interaction in product development / Jens Laage-Hellman.
        p.   cm.
    Includes bibliographical references (p.   ) and index.
    1. Industrial marketing—Japan.   2. Industrial
procurement—Japan.   3. Business networks—Japan.
4. Strategic alliances (Business)—Japan.   5. Tōshiba,
Kabushiki Kaisha—Case studies.   6. Shin Nihon Seitetsu
Kabushiki Kaisha—Case studies.   I. Title.
HF5415. 1263.L3   1997
658.8'3'30952–dc20   96–16039
                                                             CIP

ISBN 0–415–14869–3

Contents

Figures

Preface

In 1991 I was offered the opportunity to spend half a year as a visiting research fellow at Hitotsubashi University's Institute of Business Research in Tokyo. During the preceding ten years I had been involved in a number of research and consulting studies on marketing, purchasing and technological innovation in industrial markets. I belonged to a group of researchers at Uppsala University who for many years had devoted themselves to the study of industrial (i.e., business-to-business) markets. As a result of this research, which to a large extent had been carried out in cooperation with colleagues from Sweden and other European countries, a so-called interaction and network approach to the study of industrial markets had been developed. I had used this approach as a theoretical framework for studies of technological innovation in several fields, such as specialty steel, biotechnology and medical devices. In parallel, technological development in other industries had been investigated by some of my colleagues.

In accordance with the chosen framework the main theme in this research concerned how various 'industrial actors', such as selling and buying firms, interacted with each other in the context of technological innovation. Some studies focused on the interaction taking place within individual business relationships, others focused on the pattern of technological development in networks of connected relationships. Among other results, our research showed that for buyers and sellers of industrial goods technological cooperation with various kinds of partners is an important element in the development and commercialization of new products and new manufacturing processes. Therefore, the issue of how companies, as sellers or buyers, should manage their external interaction with other 'industrial actors' in the surrounding network is an important and relevant field of study.

When planning the research to be carried out in Japan, it was a natural choice for me to use the industrial network approach in order to study how Japanese companies interact in situations similar to those we had investigated previously. Since at the time I happened to be somewhat involved in a Swedish study of engineering ceramics and powder metallurgy, I saw certain advantages in choosing materials development as my topic in the Japanese study too. Thanks to the initiative of Professor Ikujiro Nonaka, my host at Hitotsubashi University and Director of the Institute of Business Research, it was possible to start up a number of case studies of product development in Japanese companies. Two of these cases – one concerned with Toshiba Corporation and one with Nippon Steel Corporation – constitute the main empirical base of the present study.

This book is thus about supplier–customer interaction in product development and aims at increasing our understanding of this phenomenon. The international dimension is an important element of the study for two reasons. First, in one of the two cases the focal cooperative relationship happened to be an international one. Second, although it is true that the research project was not designed as a comparative study, the fact that the same theoretical approach had been used in previous research on European companies gave certain opportunities to compare interacting behavior of Japanese and Western companies.

Although the book has been entirely written by myself, there are two persons who have played a key role in the project. First and foremost, it would not have been possible to carry out the study without the active support of Ikujiro Nonaka. It was thanks to his eminent contacts with the Japanese industry that I could get access to the case companies and collect the data I needed. Furthermore, throughout the entire research process he has supported me in different ways: for example, by generously giving me a lot of practical advice and sharing his broad and deep knowledge about industrial knowledge creation in general and in Japan in particular. By inviting me to stay at his institute for several shorter and longer periods from 1991 to 1994, he provided me with the best possible academic affiliation and research environment I could have had in Japan. It is not an overstatement to say that I am deeply indebted to him.

The other person who was involved in the project is Tohru Takai, then doctoral student at Waseda University and now Assistant Professor at Obirin University in Tokyo. He played an important role in the writing of the Toshiba case by helping me with the data collection. In addition, the many stimulating discussions we have had during these years have given me a lot of valuable insights and knowledge of relevance for the present study. His friendship and great hospitality also contributed to make my stay in Japan such a pleasant experience.

Besides these two individuals there are a great number of other people who in a more indirect way have contributed to the present study. As already hinted at, the stimulating and friendly atmosphere of the Institute was important to me. The contacts with other members of the permanent faculty, such as associate professors Seiichiro Yonekura, Joung-hae Seo and Tsuyoshi Numagami, just to mention a few of them, were highly appreciated. Among the other visiting researchers with whom I had fruitful discussions of relevance for the present study I would particularly like to mention the professors Michael L. Gerlach, University of California, Berkeley (USA); Michael A. Cusumano, Massachusetts Institute of Technology (USA); Leonard H. Lynn, Case Western Reserve University (USA), and doctoral students Martin Hemmert, University of Cologne (Germany) (now at the German Institute for Japanese Studies in Tokyo) and Yuncheol Lee, Seoul National University (Korea). Not to be forgotten in this context are all the secretarial and administrative staff of the Institute. They have always been very helpful to me.

Needless to say, the willingness of numerous company managers to allow interviews and spend time with me was a necessary prerequisite for the study. I am deeply indebted to all of them. In particular, I would like to mention Masato Sakai at Toshiba and Kametaro Itoh and Takashi Hada at Nippon Steel.

Especially at an early stage, the Science and Technology Office at the Swedish Embassy in Tokyo was helpful to me – for example, in arranging some visits and inviting me to various meetings. Among other persons, I would like to thank Sten Bergman, the then Science and Technology Counsellor; Akihiro Sunaga, attaché, and Yukiko Asaoka, assistant attaché.

Here follows an incomplete list of other persons from Japanese universities and companies who in various ways have contributed to my research during my stays in Japan: Gene Gregory, Sophia University; Sigvald Harrysson, Sophia University (now at Arthur D. Little Inc.); Naoto Iwasaki, Obirin University (now at Seijo University); Yoshiji Kojima, IBM Japan; Kiyofumi Matsumoto, Canon Inc.; Takebi Otsubo, Nomura School of Advanced Management; Tim Ray, National Institute for Science and Technology Policy, NISTEP (now at RIKEN); Sung-Joon Roh, NISTEP and The MIT Japan Program; Frank-Jürgen Richter, Tsukuba University (now at Robert Bosch GmbH); and Yoshiya Teramoto, Tsukuba University (now at Hokkaido University).

Back in Sweden my research in Japan has been supported by several of my former colleagues at the Department of Business Studies, Uppsala University. The most important input to the book has come from the professors Håkan Håkansson and Jan Johanson. Constructive criticism has also been put forward by Ivan Snehota, now at Stockholm School of Economics, and Mats B. Klint, University of Sundsvall. In a broader sense, my research on technological innovation in industrial markets has benefited from cooperation and fruitful discussions with many fellow researchers such as Björn Axelsson and Alexandra Waluszewski at Uppsala University, and Anders Lundgren at Stockholm School of Economics. There are many others whose names cannot be mentioned without taking the risk of being unfair.

Financial support for the research project was kindly provided by Uppsala University through The Sasakawa Young Leaders Fellowship Fund. The grant made it possible to stay in Japan as a visiting researcher several times during 1991 and 1992. Thanks to another research fellowship from the Japanese–German Center Berlin I was able spend the whole year of 1994 in Japan. It was during the beginning of that period that the book was finalized. I would like to express my gratitude to both of these institutions.

Jens Laage-Hellman
Gothenburg, January 1996

Chapter 1

Introduction

1.1 THE IMPORTANCE OF TECHNOLOGICAL COOPERATION

Our success in developing and introducing new products for the world market is not based on our own R&D capability. This is not to say that this capability is unimportant. On the contrary, it is the foundation for our long-term technology and product strategy. But another key success factor of at least equal importance is our ability to establish close cooperative links with various external partners. It is by cooperating with qualified customers, suppliers, and other advanced sources of technology that we can combine the right resources and do the right things in the right way and at the right point in time. That is how we can keep abreast with our competitors and serve our customers in the best way.

This statement by the CEO of a leading Swedish manufacturer of medical equipment illustrates an important economic phenomenon; that is, the strategic importance of inter-organizational technology cooperation in developing and commercializing industrial products.[1] In other words, new industrial goods and services are in most cases not the result of one single firm's efforts, but tend to be the outcome of an interplay among two or several companies or organizations that have different, but complementary, resources and which play different roles in the innovation process. A typical case is when a supplier and a potential user jointly develop a new product or application which is subsequently marketed to other customers.

This phenomenon is not new, and moreover it has been observed and commented on by numerous students of technological innovation and industrial development. Ample evidence of the importance of inter-organizational technological exchange can thus be found in the literature, including both economics-oriented and management-oriented studies. A few examples from the literature will be given just to illustrate what some other researchers have said about this phenomenon.

If we start with economics, it is true that to a large extent technical change has been disregarded by traditional, neoclassical economic theory, and that the creation of new technology therefore remains unexplained by this theory. But it is also true that valuable contributions to the understanding of technological innovation have come from industrial economists, especially those belonging to the Schumpeterian tradition (see, e.g., Dosi et al., 1988). Even though the main focus in this research has been on horizontal market structure and intra-industry competition, the importance of studying technical linkages between industries operating at different levels in the production chain has been emphasized by some economists (e.g., Freeman, 1982; Malerba, 1985). It has even been suggested that the interaction between users and producers should be the key to understanding the industrial innovation process and its effects on the economy (Lundvall, 1988).

Similar conclusions have been reached by Japanese economists such as Nakatani (1990) who argues that the remarkable innovativeness and economic performance of Japanese industry in the 1970s and 1980s can be attributed in large measure to the unique industrial structure of Japan. One important characteristic of this structure is the existence of close vertical and horizontal groupings among firms, which among other positive effects facilitates long-term and mutually beneficial product development cooperation between assemblers and subcontractors.

Also in economic-historical studies of innovations one can find evidence of the importance of technological exchange. The phenomenon has been observed by Nathan Rosenberg among others. In his study of the American machine tool industry, for example, he found that the interaction between machine builders and users was essential for understanding the pattern of technical change in that industry (Rosenberg, 1976).[2]

Another category of economics-oriented research, which has pointed out the role and importance of inter-organizational technological exchange, is what can be called general empirical studies of innovations. One of the more well-known studies in this category is the so-called SAPPHO project carried out by the Science Policy Research Unit at the University of Sussex (Achilladelis *et al.*, 1971; Rothwell *et al.*, 1974). In trying to identify factors which are important to the commercial success of industrial research and development (R&D) projects, they found the understanding of user needs to be the single most important success factor. Thus, successful innovators had a much better understanding of the users' requirements and tended to cooperate more often with potential customers than unsuccessful firms. Furthermore, the SAPPHO study showed that successful innovators made a more effective use of external technology and competence, and that this required not only good contacts with the scientific community and the business environment but a more directed and deeper collaboration with certain units. Results similar to the ones obtained in the SAPPHO project have been reported in other broad surveys of innovations, such as Myers and Marquis (1969) and Langrish *et al.* (1972) just to mention two other studies.

In summary, we can conclude from these studies that technological cooperation in different forms is an important phenomenon. But what is lacking to a large extent in this kind of literature are descriptions and analyses of how the technological exchange takes place. In other words, how do companies interact with each other in the development of new technology? What is the role of external relationships in the innovation process? What are the problems and difficulties? What are the positive effects that can be achieved? Let us therefore take a look at the management literature and see to what extent it can shed some light on these issues.

There is an abundant literature on the themes of 'management of technology' and 'management of innovation'. However, most of this literature focuses on intra-firm aspects of innovation and therefore pays relatively little attention to the interaction with various external parties. This fact notwithstanding, important contributions to the understanding of technological exchange have in fact been made by several management researchers, especially among those studying innovation from a marketing perspective. In his now classic studies of the sources of innovation, von Hippel (1988) showed that the users of industrial products (in contrast to the predictions offered by traditional marketing theory) often play an active role in the development of new products. Some industries are even characterized by a 'user-dominated pattern of innovation', which means that the users rather than the producers dominate the innovation process. This implies that the manufacturers should not only try to identify their customers' needs but also pay close attention to product improvements and inventions made by the customers themselves. And this requires good working relationships at the technical level.

Von Hippel's main argument, based on studies of several US high-technology industries, is that new industrial products (in contrast to consumer products) are often generated, depending on the relative ability of users and producers to appropriate the benefits of the innovation, by some user and then, at one stage of the development process, transferred to a manufacturer who takes responsibility for the further development and commercialization of the product. This view of the interplay among users and producers differs somewhat from the approach used in this book, which has its origin in European research on industrial marketing and purchasing carried out since the mid-1970s (see, e.g., Håkansson, 1982b; Ford, 1990). In studying buyer–seller relationships it was observed already at an early stage that technological exchange in many cases constituted an important element in the overall exchange process. What they saw was that ideas and technical knowledge was not only transferred between suppliers and customers, but that these firms often cooperated actively with each other in order to jointly create new technology. These observations spurred the interest in the phenomenon of technological exchange and led to the initiation of several studies focusing more specifically on technological development in industrial markets (e.g., Håkansson, 1982a and 1987b; Laage-Hellman, 1984 and 1987; Laage-Hellman and Axelsson, 1986; Axelsson, 1987; Håkansson, 1989; Waluszewski, 1989; Lundgren 1991 and 1995; Håkansson et al., 1993).

Also in Japan the importance of buyer–seller relationships to technological innovation has been observed and discussed by management researchers. For example, Imai et al. (1988) emphasize that product development in Japan cannot be viewed solely as an intra-firm activity. According to them, the inter-organizational network formed between the manufacturer and its outside suppliers is an important factor behind the speed and flexibility that characterize the innovative activities of successful Japanese machinery manufacturers. These networks are characterized, inter alia, by the self-organizing way in which they emerge, the tightly knit interactions and shared division of labor among the members, and the reciprocity which results from the development of trusting relationships. Besides their collaboration with suppliers these Japanese companies also develop cooperative R&D relationships with various research institutions and affiliated companies.

Another type of technology cooperation has been described by Teramoto *et al.* (1987). They found that some small Japanese firms created a kind of formalized network in order to overcome the shortage of intra-organizational resources and the difficulty in obtaining resources necessary for R&D on the open market. If such networks are established on the principle 'one member from one industry' they are expected to be effective in promoting R&D in smaller firms.

Although the phenomenon of technological exchange is not a new one, it seems that the awareness of its importance has increased in recent years. And this seems to be true especially for the United States, where traditionally the interest has more often centered on the role of competition; for example, when addressing the issue of industrial development and competitiveness. In a study carried out a few years ago by the MIT Commission on Industrial Productivity it was concluded that increasing industrial cooperation, both vertically and horizontally, is one of the keys to improving the performance of the American industry (Dertouzos *et al.*, 1989). The lack of cooperation between firms and their suppliers and customers is seen as one of the main factors behind the weak competitiveness of American industry. The Commission therefore recommends the US companies to establish closer cooperative relationships and joint R&D with suppliers and customers as a means to encourage technological innovation and productivity growth.

The role of inter-firm cooperation as a conduit for technological innovation has attracted growing interest, not only among economists and management researchers but also in the business press where the significance of cooperative relationships has been highlighted more often in recent years. For example, in a cover story published in January 1992, *Business Week* describes how US companies during the past six years have tried to learn from Japan by creating their own homegrown *keiretsu* (i.e., the type of tight corporate groupings that are found in Japan). Inspired by the successful business practices pursued by Japanese companies, the article says, hundreds of American firms 'are revamping their cultures and recasting their investment practices to form cooperative links both vertically, down their supply lines, and horizontally, with universities, research labs, and their peers' (p. 38). This changing behavior is said to indicate the emergence of a new US industrial pattern where horizontal and vertical cooperation plays a much more important role than in the past. This happens partly because the American companies perceive the value of collaborating closely with suppliers and customers on research and production to be an advantage they can no longer afford to ignore if they are to compete successfully with their foreign counterparts.

Strong evidence of the strategic importance of technological cooperation among firms can thus be found in the literature, including both academic publications and other less scientific sources. However, as already hinted at, there is a need for more in-depth inquiry into this phenomenon in order to better understand how the technological exchange among companies takes place and how it can be managed to foster industrial innovativeness and competitiveness. It is within this problem context that the present study has been carried out.

1.2 PURPOSE OF THE STUDY AND CONTENT OF THE BOOK

As follows from the preceding section, this book is concerned with technological cooperation – primarily between selling and buying firms in industrial markets. It is based on a study carried out in Japan during 1991 and 1992. The core consists of two longitudinal in-depth case studies of material innovations. One case deals with Nippon Steel Corporation's development of coated steel sheet for autobodies and focuses primarily on this company's cooperation with a key customer, Toyota Motor Corporation. The other case describes Toshiba Corporation's development and commercialization of advanced ceramics for structural use. An important part of this development work has been carried out in collaboration with an American customer, Cummins Engine Company.

The empirical purpose of the study was to investigate how Nippon Steel and Toshiba had interacted with their respective key partners and other external units in the development and commercialization of these products. There are several generally applicable research questions that can be addressed within the frame of such a study. For example, why do companies choose to perform technological development in cooperation with others? How do they select their partners? What kind of problems and difficulties do they encounter during the cooperation, and how can these problems be solved? What are the positive and negative effects of the cooperation? These questions are undoubtedly relevant from a management point of view. Therefore, by describing and analyzing the two cases the study aims at generating some useful knowledge about these questions and their answers, and by so doing enhancing the understanding of the innovation process.

Since the early 1980s a number of innovation studies, using as theoretical framework 'an industrial interaction and network approach', have been carried out in Europe (e.g., Håkansson, 1987a; Håkansson, 1989; Laage-Hellman, 1989; Waluszewski, 1989; Lundgren, 1991 and 1995; Shaw, 1991; Biemans 1992). Even though the present research is not thought of as a comparative study, the existence of these previous and other ongoing studies provides an opportunity to make at least some tentative comparisons between interacting and networking behavior in different industrial environments; i.e., primarily between Japan and Europe. It should be made clear, however, that this was not one of the main purposes of the study.

In Chapter 2 the above-mentioned interaction and network approach to the study of industrial markets, which constitutes the main theoretical point of departure, is introduced. The research methodology, in terms of the practical realization of the study, is briefly described in Chapter 3. The two cases are then described and commented on in Chapters 4 and 5 respectively. The result of the case analysis is presented in Chapter 6. To conclude, some international differences and similarities in interacting and networking behavior are discussed in Chapter 7.

Chapter 2

Technological development in industrial markets
An interaction and network approach

2.1 THE CONCEPT OF BUSINESS RELATIONSHIPS

More than fifteen years of research on industrial markets (also called 'business-to-business markets') has proved the importance, richness and diversity of buyer–seller relationships (see, e.g., Håkansson, 1982b; Turnbull and Valla, 1986; Ford, 1990; Gadde and Håkansson, 1993; Håkansson and Snehota, 1995). As demonstrated by numerous studies a large share of the business transactions in such markets takes place within long-lasting buyer–seller relationships that are often stable, close and complex in nature. In contrast to the assumptions made in the traditional marketing theory (see, e.g., Kotler, 1988) both buyers and sellers are active in initiating and developing business exchange. Furthermore, the individual buyers are often large and powerful and have specific identities and different needs. This makes it necessary for the seller to deal with many of its customers on an individual basis (instead of seeing them as anonymous and 'faceless' buyers which together make up a homogeneous segment of the market).

According to this approach to industrial marketing and purchasing, which is extensively described in the above-mentioned references, the key problem encountered by selling as well as purchasing companies has to do with the establishment, development and handling of business relationships. In other words, the long-term effectiveness and performance of the company is largely dependent on how well it manages its relationships with suppliers, customers and other business partners.

Buyer–seller relationships (or 'business relationships' used as a synonym here) thus constitute core elements in industrial markets. They can be defined as exchange relationships between autonomous business units.

Exchange may refer to ordinary business exchange but it may also include communication or any ongoing relation where autonomous business units give to and receive from each other. Business units are firms or parts of firms having some kind of free choice whether or not to continue exchange with each other.
(Håkansson and Johanson, 1993, p. 14)

Besides customer and supplier relationships firms may have other exchange relationships which are important to their business activities. For example, firms may have reasons to develop more or less close and long-lasting relationships with customers' customers, suppliers' suppliers, competitors and manufacturers of complementary products (who sell to the same customers). Figure 2.1 illustrates schematically how a mechanical engineering company can be related to other companies through different kinds of relationships. Furthermore, in connection to technical development projects it may be useful to establish relationships with, for example, research institutions, development companies, consultants and governmental agencies.

The extensive research on business relationships that has been carried out in different parts of the world during the last two decades has produced a picture of such relationships that converges

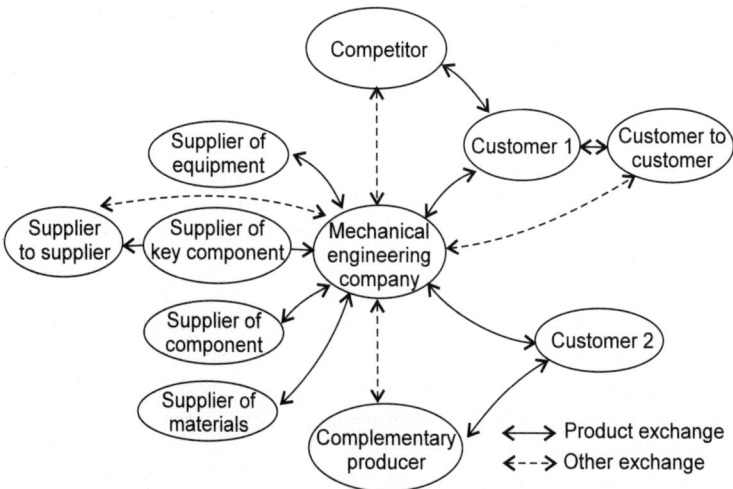

Figure 2.1 Example of a company network
Source: Gadde and Håkansson (1993)

on a few recurrent characteristics. In summarizing these findings Håkansson and Snehota (1995, Ch. 1) distinguish between structural and process characteristics. In regard to the former, they point out that business relationships are often characterized by continuity, complexity, symmetry and informality. Major supplier and customer relationships of a company thus tend to show a striking continuity and relative stability. Relationships 10–20 years old are not unusual. The complexity of business relationships can be seen in several ways, for example in terms of the number and type of individuals involved and the use of relationships for multiple purposes. Unlike the typical situation in many consumer markets the relationships in industrial markets are often characterized by a more symmetrical distribution of resources and capabilities. Thus, the buyers are often strong and active. A fourth structural characteristic of business relationships is that they often show a low degree of formalization. Informal mechanisms, based on trust and confidence, are often more effective for the development of relationships than formal contractual arrangements.

The fact that companies in industrial markets tend to be tied to each other by apparently long-lasting, broad, balanced and informal relationships should not be interpreted as a lack of dynamism. On the contrary, continuous change is a normal feature of every significant business relationship. The previous research has pointed out four typical process characteristics of business relationships: adaptations, cooperation and conflict, social interaction, and routinization. Mutual adaptations, reflecting a need for coordination of activities, occur in many relationships and are often a prerequisite for fruitful, long-term development. The coexistence of an atmosphere of cooperation and conflict has been found to be a normal element in all business relationships. Social interaction plays an important role in most business relationships. The latter are generally built up as a social exchange process in which individuals learn to know and trust each other and make commitments going beyond the immediate task. Despite the fact that business relationships are often complex and informal in nature, they tend to become institutionalized over time. Thus, specific routines, roles of behavior, etc., often emerge within more important relationships.

After this short summary of some important characteristics of business relationships a model for describing and analyzing relationships in terms of interaction processes will be presented. The model, illustrated in Figure 2.2, consists of three main parts: the

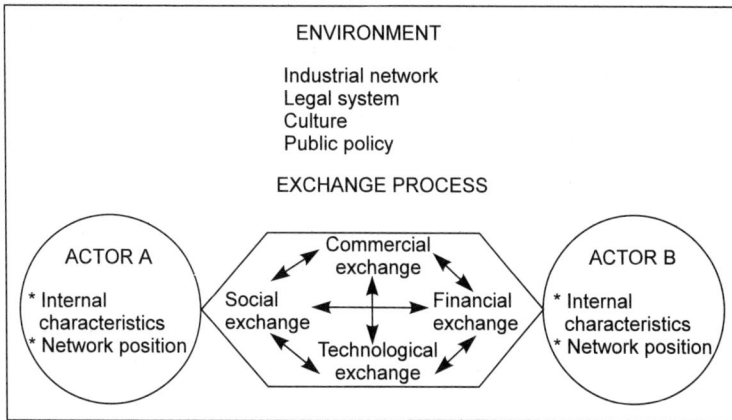

Figure 2.2 Interaction model

exchange process, the actors, and the environment. The relationship between the two actors A and B is the result of an exchange process (i.e., the interaction), which in its turn is affected by the characteristics of the actors and the environment.[1]

The exchange process

An exchange can be said to take place when two industrial actors (e.g., a seller and a buyer) consciously interact with each other in order to transfer resources and/or perform some activity together. The exchange process is complex and multidimensional in nature. The commercial, technological, social, and financial exchanges constitute the main dimensions. As illustrated by the figure, these four dimensions are not independent of each other but constitute integrated aspects of the overall exchange process.

Needless to say, the *commercial exchange* is the core of buyer–seller relationships. Besides the transfer of goods or services in exchange for money or some other form of payment, the commercial exchange itself (in a narrow sense) may in addition include the transfer of other resources such as information, knowledge and proprietary rights.

Technological exchange, broadly defined, comprises all those exchange activities which affect the techniques used or produced by the two parties. The scope of this exchange may thus vary within broad limits. It can be anything from a one-shot transfer of a small piece of information to an extensive joint R&D project in which both parties invest large resources over a considerable period of time.

The technological exchange between a supplier and a customer is more or less closely related to the commercial exchange. It is part of the total business exchange and serves to support, facilitate, or even allow, the accomplishment of commercial transactions. For example, the supplier and the customer may exchange technical information or carry out joint development activities in order to adapt product designs or bring about entirely new technical solutions in response to new customer demands or new technical possibilities.

In other types of relationships, the technological exchange *per se* may be the primary purpose of the relationship. This is the case, for example, when industrial firms interact with universities, research institutes and development companies. Furthermore, technology development may be the main reason for establishing direct relationships with companies belonging to the same industry or producing complementary products.

Financial exchange means that one company acquires shares in another firm or grants long-term credits or loans to that firm. The transaction can be one-sided or mutual. The financial tie established in this way contributes a certain degree of stability and long-sightedness to the relationship, which may facilitate the performance of other exchanges. For example, by reducing the uncertainty about the future relationship the parties may become more inclined to engage in risky and long-term cooperative projects. Ownership can also provide a power base which can be used by companies to influence the partners, such as forcing them to carry out certain activities that they otherwise would not do.

Neither commercial, technological nor financial exchange can take place unless there are at least some personal contacts between individuals representing the interacting companies. In other words, there is always a *social dimension*. Its importance varies from relationship to relationship, and also over time within individual relationships. Social interaction is important in itself when carrying out certain exchange activities; for example, when delivering certain types of services, transferring skills and knowledge, and when negotiating business deals. However, maybe more important in the long run is that in the course of the exchange process the people involved gradually learn to know each other. Under favorable conditions a mutual trust and friendship is built. Like the financial exchange, the social exchange has an important function in reducing the uncertainty between the actors. By creating social ties between the individuals, and thereby interlocking the companies with each other, the relationship is stabilized. This may facilitate or even be a prerequisite for other types of exchange.

The social dimension is important, especially in connection with technological development. It is so partly because of the 'tacitness' which characterizes much of the industrial technology. Tacit knowledge, that by definition is tied to and difficult to separate from individuals, cannot be easily articulated. It is because the individuals capable of doing certain things are not themselves fully aware of the details of the performance. As a consequence, tacit knowledge is difficult to transfer outside of its context. It must to a large extent be acquired through learning by doing, and cannot be exchanged between organizations without involving the individuals who possess it. One way of transferring tacit knowledge is to let individuals from two organizations work together (e.g., within a joint project). But in order to make this knowledge exchange effective the individuals have to build trustful personal relations, and this can only be done through a social process (which can take place partly on the job, partly after working hours).

It should be noted that social contacts and the building of trustful relationships are important to the technological exchange also because of the genuine uncertainty which to a higher or lower degree characterizes all innovation processes. One cannot know in advance exactly what will be needed to achieve a certain goal, or if it can be reached at all. It is impossible to make formal contracts that cover all problems and difficulties that might come up. Instead, technological cooperation must, to a large extent, be founded on mutual trust and expectations that unforeseeable problems will be solved in a cooperative spirit.

To summarize this discussion, it can be concluded that the commercial, technological, financial, and social exchanges constitute different aspects of the overall exchange process which takes place within the relationship. The different types of exchanges are linked with and dependent on one another and cannot be seen as separate processes. To understand one type of exchange, for example the technological, it is therefore not enough to analyze only that form of exchange. It is also necessary to examine how that exchange is related to other aspects of the total relationship.

An important effect of the exchange is that different kinds of bonds, links and ties are created – for example, technical, logistical, organizational, financial, legal, and social. Bonds, links and ties are key elements in the analytical network model of relationships and will be explained in more detail later on. The degree of bonding in a relationship can be seen as a measure of its strength and long-term stability.

The actors

How the interaction process develops in a certain relationship is not only dependent on the elements exchanged (e.g., what type of products or technologies) and the degree of bonding, but also on the attributes of the actors themselves. As illustrated in Figure 2.2 the model distinguishes between *internal characteristics* and *network position*. The former can be described in terms of:

- the resources possessed or controlled by the actor (physical assets, labor, knowledge, financial means, etc.),
- the production and other resource-transforming activities performed by the actor,
- the organizational structure by which the resources and activities are organized, and
- the objectives and strategies pursued by the actor.

The similarities and differences in the actors' resource and activity structures give the basic conditions for exchange. This is obvious in the case of buyer–seller relationships. The logic behind the establishment of such relationships is the need for utilizing and handling complementarities between the supplier's and the customer's production systems. What is exchanged, and how, is thus strongly dependent on the resources and activities of each party. For example, the availability of internal R&D resources and the direction of ongoing development activities not only determine what a certain company wants to obtain from other actors (e.g., suppliers or customers) but also what that company can offer in return.

The organizational structure can be described in such terms as the degree of centralization, specialization and formalization. The structure influences not only the internal functioning of the firm but also how it interacts with external parties; for example, which individuals and departments that take part in exchange activities, the way of communicating with external units, the openness toward others, and the emphasis placed on formal agreements. The establishment of a fruitful exchange is facilitated if the actors have organizational structures and business cultures which match each other in a suitable way.

The same can be said about the objectives and strategies pursued by the actors. Mutuality – that is, that actors are prepared to interact with each other and expect each other to do so – is a precondition for the establishment of a fruitful relationship. And this mutuality can be the result of a certain complementarity between the objectives and strategies. Each firm may seek to gain different, but consistent, gains from the cooperation (e.g., the acquisition of a new resource and access to a new market respectively), or the goal of the interaction might be commonly held (e.g., developing a new technology that both are interested in).

The network position has to do with the actor's position in relation to its environment. As will be described in the next section the industrial system to which the company belongs can be seen as a network of relationships among firms. These relationships are connected, which means that the exchange that takes place in one relationship affects and is affected by what is happening in certain other relationships in which the two interacting parties are involved. In every relationship there is a natural tension between cooperation and conflict. This tension is very much related to the existence of connections. For example, a confliction of interests between a seller and a buyer may have its origin in the buyer's relationship with another supplier or the seller's relationship with another customer.

How each of the two actors are linked up with the surrounding network is thus important for the exchange that takes place in the focal relationship. This linkage can be described in terms of network position defined in the following way:

1 The identity of those other actors with which the focal actor has direct or indirect relationships.
2 The characteristics of these specific relationships (the existence of different kinds of exchanges and bonds).

Each actor has some kind of unique position in the network, which is the result of its previous interactions with various counterparts. This position is never static but changes continuously as a result of the exchange activities which take place in the network.

The environment

The interaction between two actors takes place within a wider context, which may affect the relationship in various ways. The environment is here described in terms of the surrounding industrial network, the national culture, the legal system, and the public policy.

The industrial market in which both actors are operating is viewed as a network of relationships where companies are linked to one another through two-party exchange relationships. As already pointed out, these relationships are connected, which as a matter of fact is a precondition for using the network metaphor (otherwise the market would only consist of a bundle of independent dyads).

The connectedness of relationships thus implies the existence of an aggregated structure, a form of 'organization', that can be labeled as network. Relationships are in other words part of a broader structure as much as the companies can be viewed as elements of such a structure. This assumption is important since it leads to a different picture of the role and potential of business firms, how industrial markets function, and the means by which the company can be managed. One of the peculiar features of the network form of organization is that it differs from the 'hierarchy', in which components are assumed to be invariably linked, and from the 'market', with its atomistic structure (Håkansson and Snehota, 1995).

The industrial network also differs from other network concepts, such as for example social or communication networks, in that the actors are involved in the economic processes which convert resources to finished goods and services for consumption by end-users, whether they be individuals or firms (Axelsson and Easton, 1992, p. xiv). Thus, the linkages between actors are defined, as already described, in terms of economic exchanges which are themselves conducted within the framework of enduring relationships. In other words, the existence of such relationships are the *raison d'être* for industrial networks. They provide the stability, and hence structure, which makes the network metaphor particularly apposite (*ibid.*).

The network approach can be seen as a new paradigm for industrial markets and thereby provides an alternative to the traditional microeconomics-based models for marketing and purchasing management. In contrast to the latter, according to which buying as well as selling firms are assumed to be free and independent units in a market characterized by an atomistic structure and clear boundaries, each company is here viewed as an integrated part of a network with arbitrary boundaries. Each actor is also characterized by strong dependencies on other actors in the network. These dependencies can be specific (i.e., linked to individual interaction partners), or general (i.e., caused by the actors' involvement in the network as such). Another difference from the conventional market model is that all actors are assumed to be different. That is, the network is heterogeneous both with regard to the sellers' offers and the buyers' needs (in markets, by contrast, offers and needs are assumed to be homogeneous within the respective segment).

In the following section a conceptual framework for analyzing exchange relationships in a network perspective will be outlined in more detail.

Besides the characteristics of the network, which constitute the most important part of the environment and affect the focal relationship through connections with other relationships, the interaction is also influenced by other more general environmental factors such as the national culture, the legal system and the public policy.

How people view and interact with each other when doing business may thus be influenced by the culture of the country in which the actors are situated. If in a certain society, for example, people are considered to be good and inclined to trust each other,[2] one would expect this cultural feature to facilitate the establishment of cooperative relationships among firms. Furthermore, if two interacting companies come from different cultural environments communication problems may arise due to, for example, differences in mental frames of reference, social manners and business practices.

The legal system may have an effect on the interaction between two companies; for example, by prohibiting certain types of contacts and cooperation. The American anti-trust legislation is a good example. Governments can also use other policy measures to influence how actors interact with each other. For example, the industrial or technology policy of a certain country (or international community) can have elements directed at stimulating cooperation between certain types of actors. One of the main objectives of nationally and internationally funded R&D programs is often to link certain types of actors with each other (e.g., companies and research units, users and producers, different companies within the same industry, etc.).

2.2 A NETWORK-BASED FRAMEWORK FOR DESCRIPTION AND ANALYSIS OF BUSINESS RELATIONSHIPS[3]

The notion of 'relationship' has been chosen to characterize the exchange and interaction that takes place between companies in industrial markets (networks). This choice is based on a substantial amount of empirical research results. While it is certainly true that relationships do not exist in the real world (nobody has ever seen or touched a relationship), these results indicate that the business exchange between selling and buying firms often occurs in the form of an interaction that is broader, thicker and more long-term than the discrete and unrelated economic transactions described in the traditional marketing textbook. In other words, there are good reasons for using a concept of relationship that evokes mutual orientation, commitment over time, and interdependence. These features of relationships constrain the companies' freedom of action as much as they create opportunities. Relationships can thus be demanding and problematic besides being mutually rewarding.

It is true that each relationship has unique characteristics. But what they have in common is the complexity of the intervening variables. As suggested by Håkansson and Snehota (1995) this complex nature of relationships can be caught by using two traits or dimensions that appear to be common to all business relationships – namely, the substance of exchange and the plurality of functions. The former regards what is affected and the latter who is affected.

The substance of relationships

The substance of a relationship (e.g., between a supplier and a customer) varies with the total volume of exchange and the variety of exchange elements that make up the value of the relationship. Three different layers of substance can be identified. They are concerned with actors, activities and resources, which are the three basic elements of the industrial network model.

Resources represent a necessary condition for all industrial activities. In the case of the individual company, five basic types of resources can be identified, each related to some part of the environment. They are input goods, financial capital, technology, personnel, and marketing channels. These resources, the importance of which may vary over time, can be controlled by the company in two different ways: either directly by owning the resource or the right to use it; or indirectly by having close relationships with other actors who possess the formal control.

A typical feature of resources is that they are heterogeneous; that is, the value or utility of a particular resource depends on with which other resources it is combined. This also means that the value is not constant. By finding more efficient ways to combine it with other resources (e.g., through technological cooperation), the value can be increased. Learning about resources, the company's own as well as those of others, is thus important. For example, new insights into the properties of resources and the possibilities to make new combinations can contain the seeds for technological innovation and network change.

Activities are carried out within and between individual actors and tie resources to each other. Two main kinds of activities can be distinguished: production or transformation activities and exchange activities. Figure 2.3 illustrates schematically how single activities can be seen as links in longer activity chains in the network. It indicates how the various exchange and production activities, being parts in a larger whole, depend on certain other activities having taken place before and how they provide the basis for other exchange and production activities further downstream in the chain. Because of these dependencies a single change in one activity always has some effect, great or small, on other activities in the network.

A single production activity often belongs to several activity chains (or even several networks) at the same time. That means that the way of performing the activity must be a compromise between the different, often conflicting, demands for adaptation made by the different chains, and the demands deriving from the internal nature of the activity as well. There will always be reasons to question this compromise. Therefore, the function of relationships (exchange activities) is not only to bridge the gaps between different production activities but also to channel and handle a variety of conflicting forces in the network.

Actors exist at different organizational levels. They can, for example, be individuals, departments, business units, firms, and

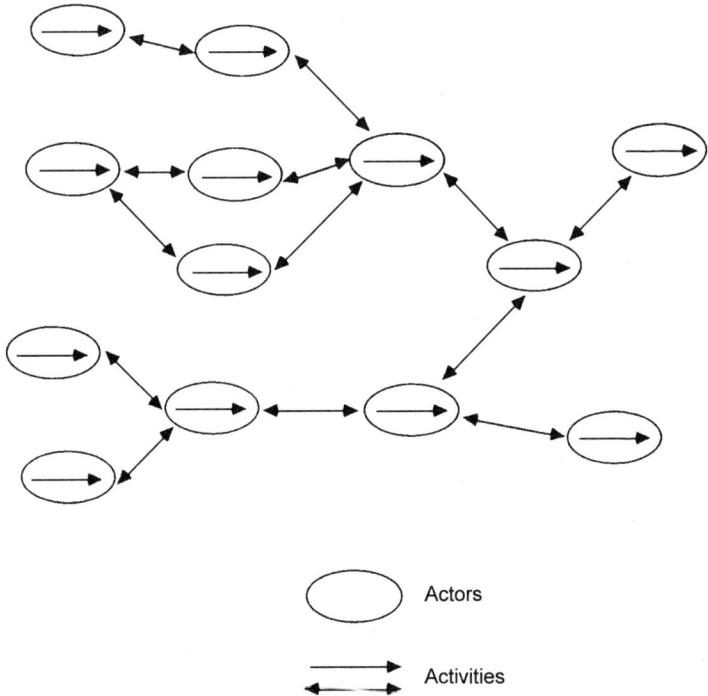

Figure 2.3 Schematic illustration of a network

groups of firms. Actors at lower levels are usually part of higher level actors.

Each actor is embedded in a network of more or less strong relationships, which gives it access to other actors' resources. These resources, in combination with those over which the actor has direct control, are used to perform various activities and achieve certain goals. The general goal of the actors is supposed to be to increase their control over the network. This follows from the assumption that control can be used to achieve other more specific goals, such as profit, growth, market share, excellence, prestige, etc.

Every actor is characterized by a unique combination of resources, activities, links and interests. Every actor therefore also faces a unique combination of demands and opportunities which affect how it acts in the network and how it reacts to the actions of others.

Another important characteristic of industrial actors is their resource-dependence. As a matter of fact the existence of the actor is totally dependent on the investments it has made in production equipment, technology, personnel and, not least, relationships with external parties. At the same time the actor is captive of these investments, since they constitute important constraints in terms of changing the activities. To change the resource structure is in most cases costly. Therefore, in the face of any demand to change the activities, the actor will always first look for the possibility to use the existing resources differently.

Activities, resources and actors constitute the three layers of exchange substance. First, a relationship, which in itself consists of activities, can link the two actors' activities in different ways. This results in various types of *activity links*, such as technical, logistical and administrative. The technical ones arise, for example, in buyer–seller relationships when one or both of the firms make adaptations in their products or production processes. The purpose is to link the two production systems to each other and in so doing make the commercial exchange more efficient. Logistical and administrative links can, for instance, be the result of the installation of common logistical or planning systems.

The result of the linking is that the activities become adapted and coordinated, which in its turn can have a number of positive effects on the companies' performance, such as their productivity and capacity. Activity links can also be important for the technological development; for example, through adaptation of development direction and target specifications, through division of labor in the R&D work, and through joint development projects. In that way the innovative performance of both companies can be enhanced.

The second substance layer consists of *resource ties*. These arise when companies tie various resource elements needed and controlled by them (e.g., raw materials, products, manufacturing equipment, technology, manpower, financial means, etc.). By bringing together, confronting and combining resources within a relationship, the resources become more or less oriented toward each other. The relationship can then be regarded as a resource in itself, since it can be used by a company to access certain resources, tangible or intangible, that it needs for its operations.

Resource ties are particularly important from a technological development point of view, since they can constitute an interface between different kinds of knowledge bodies. For example, by combining a supplier's product and production knowledge with a customer's knowledge about the use of the product, the relationship can give opportunities to develop new technical solutions that strengthen the competitiveness of both firms.

The third type of substance layer, *actor bonds*, arise when actors become mutually committed to each other, i.e., they direct a certain amount of attention, interest and priority toward each other. A bond, like the previously discussed links and ties, may be created through exchange taking place within one major business transaction, such as the execution of a big order. But more often bonds, like links and ties, are created through a series of short exchange episodes whereby the bond is gradually, sometimes unconsciously, built up. It is a process over time which typically involves mutual learning and the creation of trust between individuals through social interaction and experience of past performance.

Legal bonds in the form of written contracts can be another, more formalized, way of binding two actors to each other. Formal agreements of this kind often have a complementary or supporting function in relation to other bonds, ties and links. For example, a company may be reluctant to get engaged in a more extensive cooperation with another firm unless there is some kind of formal contract which manifests the relationship.

The actor bonds contribute to shape the identities of the actors (both in relation to each other and in the eyes of third parties) and consequently affect how these perceive, evaluate and treat each other. Behaviors in relationships are thus largely based on the assumed identity of the counterpart.

The nature and strength of actor bonds may affect the technological exchange between two companies in various ways. For example, any decision to engage in joint development with another firm will be affected by the assumed identity of that firm (e.g., if it is regarded as a 'close friend' or belongs to 'the same family').

The three layers of substance described above can be taken as three different outcome parameters as they are key determinants of the value of a relationship. A relationship between two firms can thus be characterized by the features and relative importance of the three layers of activity links, resource ties and actor bonds. So if we are to explain what is happening, or can be made to happen, in a particular relationship the existing links, ties and bonds have to be explored.

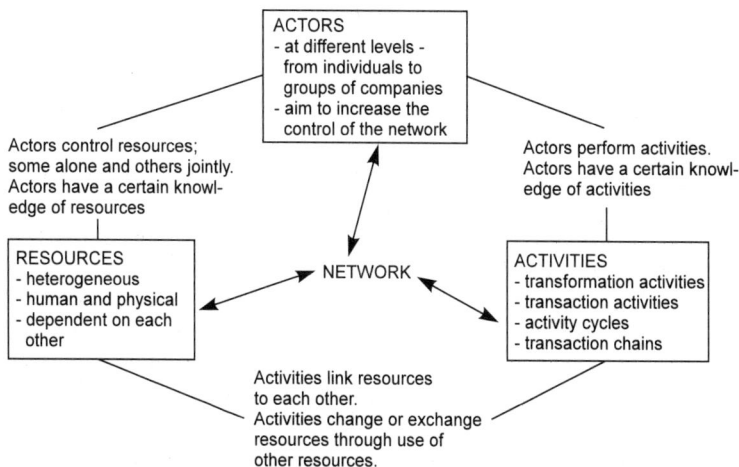

Figure 2.4 Network model
Source: Håkansson (1987a, p.17)

The three layers of relationship substance are not independent of each other. As illustrated by Figure 2.4 there are important interconnections between actors, activities and resources. As explained by Håkansson (1989):

> Actors are defined by their performance of activities and their control over resources. Activities are performed by actors, a process during which certain resources are used in order that others should be refined. And, finally, resources are controlled by actors and their value is determined by the activity in which they are used.
>
> (Håkansson, 1989, pp. 16–17)

The existence of bonds between actors is therefore a prerequisite for development of strong activity links and resource ties.

The functions of relationships

A relationship between two firms can have more than one purpose or function. This has to do with the fact that relationships constitute elements in a larger aggregated structure – the industrial network. It is a structure that consists of an 'organized' set of conscious and goal-seeking actors; but it is also an 'organized' pattern of activities and an 'organized' constellation of resources. (It should be noted that a network is not an organization in the sense of having a clear boundary or any center or apex, but exists as 'organization' more in terms of a certain logic that affects the ordering and linking of activities and tying of resources.)

First of all, the relationship always has a specific function in itself as a dyad (i.e. the two actors jointly). The relationship is a 'place' for exchange and co-action where it generates some performance – for example, with regard to commercial exchange or technological development. The relationship can therefore be said to have a 'team function', which means that the resources and activities of the two counterparts can be combined in a unique and fruitful way. But the extent to which there will be any value creating team effect is dependent on the substance of the relationship. All the three dimensions will then be important in creating a team function. This will normally develop over time as the relationship is given more substance in the form of activity links, resource ties and actor bonds.

Second, the relationship has a function for the individual actor itself; it is a resource that can be used for various purposes in combination with other internal and external resources controlled by the company. Through its substance in the form of activity links, resource ties and actor bonds, the relationship can be used to improve the actor's productivity, innovativeness and identity in the network. These effects can in turn contribute to the accumulation of resources; i.e., the overall goal of the actor according to the network approach. Relationships thus have an important 'development function' for the individual company.

Third, since the relationship is a component in an aggregated structure it also has a function for third parties and, consequently, for the network as a whole. The third parties may be affected by the relationship while at the same time the relationship is subject to forces stemming from them.

The essence of the network function is that as relationships are established and evolve they form a structure of activities, ties and bonds which affects third parties directly or indirectly through various connections. How the relationship substance develops and unfolds is thus important for the network structure and its stability or dynamism. At the same time, the properties of the emergent network structure imply limitations as well as possibilities for the development of individual relationships and actors.

An important implication of the three different functions discussed here is that the outcomes of a relationship for a certain company will not only depend on the company's own action in specific exchange episodes. The outcomes will also be affected by how the interaction partner acts and reacts and furthermore by the actions of other, connected network actors. The effect of the relationship is, in other words, a product of the different intervening functions it has for the dyad, for the individual company and for the third parties.

Basically, the dyadic function is value creating and thus a condition for realizing the 'development function' for the single actor. The network function mainly reflects the interdependence between individual and collective action. For the individual actor there is a problem of balancing the different functions, since these can sometimes be counterproductive (for example, too much emphasis on the single actor function may be detrimental to the dyadic team function; and disregard for the network function may produce negative consequences for the company). This means that coping successfully with relationships requires some ability within the company to control and manage the various functions.

Summary of the conceptual framework

As it has been described above, business, and other inter-organizational relationships in industrial markets, is a complex phenomenon with many facets, which is reflected by the complexity of factors that intervene in the development of a relationship between two actors. It has been argued that relationships develop as a consequence of the interacting parties' behavior (they are enacted). But at the same time, while free to pursue their own aims, the companies are severely constrained by others in attempting to achieve these goals through acting in the network.

It has also been argued that relationships are complex in terms of their substance and their functions and therefore in terms of the forces that affect the outcome of exchange. These two dimensions can be combined to form a model of analysis that captures the key variables intervening in the development of relationships (Figure 2.5). The nine cells in the matrix identify the dimensions in which effects are likely to occur as a relationship evolves.

The significance of this framework is that activity links in a certain relationship affect the productivity of the company and

FUNCTIONS

		Individual actor	Dyadic	Network
	Activities	Productivity	Activity links	Activity pattern
SUBSTANCE	Resources	Innovativeness	Resource ties	Resource constellation
	Actors	Identity	Actor bonds	Network organization

Figure 2.5 Summary of the conceptual framework for analysis of inter-
company relationships in industrial networks

the overall activity pattern of the industrial network; resource ties
affect the company's innovativeness and the network's resource
constellation; actor bonds, finally, affect the identity of the company and the network organization. At the same time, though, the
activity pattern of the network affects the possibility to establish
activity links and thereby to increase the productivity of the company; the resource constellation affects the possibility to create
resource ties and to enhance the company's innovativeness; the
structure of the network affects the possibility to build up actor
bonds and to shape the identity of the firm. The same type of
reasoning can be applied to the interrelatedness of the different
substance layers. Productivity, innovativeness and identity are thus
interrelated as well as the activity pattern, the resource constellation and the network organization.

2.3 NETWORKS, RELATIONSHIPS AND TECHNOLOGICAL DEVELOPMENT

According to the interaction and network approach industrial
technological development takes place as an interplay among
actors who belong to a network of relationships. This view con-
trasts with the traditional view, encountered for example in much
of the management of innovation literature, according to which
technological development mainly takes place within firms. It is the
efficiency and effectiveness of the internal technological development activities that determine how successful a company becomes.

But if the company is seen as an integrated actor in a network, this is not enough and maybe not even the most important factor for success. Then, successful innovation is largely dependent on how the company's technological development activities are related to what is happening in the surrounding network, and furthermore how this network as a whole develops. In other words, the crucial question is not how the company manages its technological development activities *per se*, but rather how it succeeds in relating its own technological development activities to what is happening inside and between other actors, such as customers and suppliers.

In the introductory chapter references were made to some studies supporting the view that technological cooperation between companies is a key element in the innovation process. Empirical research based on the interaction and network approach has shown that much of the technological development in industrial markets takes place within more or less long-lasting and stable relationships. Besides a large number of case studies, quantitative evidence is given in Håkansson's (1989 and 1990) study of 123 small and medium-sized Swedish companies (including subsidiaries and divisions of large corporations). He found that on average close to half of the R&D resources were committed to collaborative projects with various types of external parties. However, the relative share of collaboration varies a lot. The highest profitability and growth rates were obtained by companies that had about a 50 percent external share. Håkansson also found that customers and suppliers together made up almost three-quarters of the cooperation partners. It can thus be concluded that business relationships are extremely important from a technological development point of view. Among other results reported in this study, it can be mentioned that cooperative relationships with suppliers and customers tended to be more than five years old and that most of these collaborative activities took place within non-formalized relationships.

The effects of technological exchange

It has been argued that firms engage in technological exchange with other actors in order to handle various kinds of dependencies in the network. But what are, more specifically, the effects of the technological exchange? There are, as will be described, effects related to all of the three main functions of a relationship, i.e. for the dyad itself, for the individual actor and for the network.

With regard to the dyad the main effect of the technological exchange in business relationships, which will be in focus here, is to make the commercial exchange between the two parties more efficient and effective. This can be achieved in different ways; e.g., through sharing of information that enables the respective actor to adapt its own technological activities according to the needs, wishes or requirements of the counterpart; through division of development tasks and exchange of the results; and through joint R&D activities aimed at developing something, such as a method, product or application, that both are interested in (in the capacity of manufacturer or user). There are several types of exchange elements that to a larger or lesser extent can be involved in this exchange. Of paramount importance, of course, is knowledge in various forms. Some information is 'explicit', such as quantitative data, product specifications and designs, codified procedures, etc. Such information can usually be easily transferred between companies. Other knowledge is 'tacit' in its nature and therefore, as already pointed out, difficult to formalize and communicate (Nonaka, 1991). Its transfer normally requires close interaction between individuals. Other types of elements that may be involved in the technological exchange are physical products (e.g., test material and prototypes), R&D services (e.g., testing and analyzing) and proprietary rights (e.g., patents).

We can identify three types of related effects for the dyad. The most important is *knowledge creation* and it has to do with the establishment and utilization of knowledge-based resource ties. The relationship gives the opportunity to bring together different, but complementary, bodies of knowledge. If these resources are adapted to and combined with each other through interaction, this can thus lead to the development of new technology (e.g., in the form of a new or improved product). A particularly important case is when the interaction takes place between a supplier and a customer (user). The needs of the latter and its knowledge about the product use can then be directly confronted with the supplier's manufacturing know-how and knowledge about new technical solutions. In business relationships the purpose of this 'interactive effect' is normally commercial; that is, to maintain or expand the commercial exchange between the two companies. Besides the direct, short-term effect the technological exchange may also lead to a strengthening of the activity links and resource ties between the two companies' production systems. This contributes to stabilize the relationship and increase the mutual dependency between the two parties.

In other types of relationships the purpose of the cooperation may be purely technical, such as developing a technology that one or both of the actors need in order to make business with third parties. This may, for example, be the case when two firms from the same industry (e.g., two automobile manufacturers) join forces to develop common components or production methods (the underlying driving force is often economic; i.e., to exploit scale advantages in the development work).

A second dyadic effect of technological exchange in relationships is *activity coordination*, which means that the two actors mutually adapt the R&D and other relevant activities to each other. It can be with regard to time, content, goal or the way of performing and organizing the activities. Activity coordination is often a prerequisite for achieving the knowledge effects discussed above. The higher the degree of specialization in the network, the more important this function becomes.

The third effect of technological cooperation, *resource mobilization*, is also important for the knowledge creation. If there is going to be any substantial knowledge effect of the relationship both parties have to put in the necessary resources in the form of, for example, manpower, plant and laboratory capacity, and management attention. Furthermore, in order to get an invention used on a larger scale and turned into an innovation, the actors involved often have to adapt in different ways. For example, in order to take advantage of a new product's unique properties there may be a need for the customers to learn how to use the invention and combine it with other products and systems. On the seller side, it may be necessary for the supplier to put efforts into adapting, revising and redesigning the product in order to make it useful in different applications.

The interaction among the actors plays a vital role in ensuring that enough resources are mobilized when needed. This mobilization process often takes place in a context where resources are scarce and where other activities compete for the same resources. The existence of actor bonds, which implies a certain degree of mutual commitment, therefore facilitates the resource mobilization. The process of creating actor bonds and shaping the identity of the actors in the relationship is close to that of learning and involves interpretations of past behavior and performance. This explains why it often takes time to build bonds and create favorable conditions for more far-reaching technological cooperation. But at the same time the technological exchange *per se* may be used as an effective means to strengthen the bonding between two firms.

Turning to the functions of relationships for the individual actors, it can be concluded that the dyadic effects of technological exchange discussed above can be good enough for the actor. This is the case if the counterpart is a particularly important one. Then, the increased value of the relationship may be high enough to justify the efforts. However, in many cases companies seek to exploit the results of the technological exchange on a larger scale. For example, the supplier may develop a new product or application together with a specific 'lead customer' and then sell the product or application to other customers with similar needs. Such a broader exploitation of the technology may in fact be necessary in order to get a satisfactory return on the relationship-specific R&D investment. This implies the importance of regarding and evaluating individual relationships, not in isolation but in a larger context represented by the network of connected relationships.

This brings us over to the third relationship function; that is, the importance of the technological exchange for the network as a whole. Through different kinds of connections the technological exchange taking place in one relationship will have some effect, large or small depending on the circumstances, on the surrounding network. The effects may be positive in the sense that the cooperation produces new technology that increases the overall efficiency of the network (which does not exclude that certain actors are negatively affected). It should not be disregarded, however, that the establishment of a strong technical partnership between two firms can have certain negative consequences for the development of the network. If, for example, two actors are large and powerful their alliance and firm commitment to foster their own jointly developed technology may constitute an effective barrier to the introduction of other competing technologies.

As the purpose of the present study is to investigate the interaction which has taken place in two different cases of collaborative R&D, only the dyadic and the single-actor functions of relationships will be dealt with in the following. The study of network effects would require another research design.

Management and research issues

By using the interaction and network approach several important management issues relating to technological innovation can be raised. Three such broad issues, identified from the perspective of an individual company, will be discussed here. The first one has to do with the extent to which the company's innovation activities should be integrated and coordinated with various parts of the surrounding network. This issue covers several questions such as: which R&D resources and competencies should be directly controlled by the company (or business unit) and which ones should be made available through various collaborative relationships? A related question concerns which development activities should be conducted in cooperation with others and which should be carried out in-house.

Given a perceived need to have a certain degree of external technological cooperation, the next question is with what parts of the network the company should interact. For example, to what extent and for what purposes should technological cooperation be established with users, suppliers, research institutions or companies belonging to the same industry (possibly including competitors)?

It is easily recognized that the answers to these questions are contingent, to a certain extent, on the kind of industry or network the company belongs to, what position the company has in the network and the overall technology strategy. With regard to the latter, the company's long-term approach to the technological development in the network obviously has importance for the choice of cooperative approach. For example, does the company want to follow and adapt to existing patterns and trends in the network or is its goal to create new radical patterns and trends that break with the existing activity and resource structure. It is evident that different strategies in this respect require different interacting and networking behavior. Even though the industry or network characteristics, the position of the company, and its overall technology strategy have an important bearing on the choice of cooperation strategy, at the same time the latter is open to a considerable degree of freedom. In other words, how much of the development efforts should be carried out internally and in collaboration with others, respectively, is an important strategic issue in its own right.

Although many companies are well aware of the strategic importance of external cooperation and 'networking', this seems to be an issue that many companies have not paid enough attention to.

In many cases, a more conscious analysis and approach in this regard would probably contribute to the development of more effective strategies.

Given a certain cooperative approach toward the network, the company has to decide, in one way or another, with whom it should cooperate (unless it has decided to do everything in-house). This is the second management issue. One question concerns the type of collaboration partner. Within each category of counterpart (supplier, customer, etc.) potential partners usually differ with respect to, for example, size, ownership, and technology, product and market orientation. And furthermore, should there be any preferences with regard to geographical location and national belonging? Should for example priority be given to domestic partners or actors from some other country? Another question is how many partners the company should have. In other words, should the cooperation be concentrated to a few selected key partners or should parallel exchange activities be carried out with a larger number of external actors? Other questions have to do with the kind of criteria that should be used to evaluate a potential partner and the procedure by which partners are selected.

Like the previous issue, the answers will to a certain extent be given by the network characteristics, the position of the company, and the technology strategy. Needless to say, existing relationships and experiences of previous collaborative projects constitute an important starting point in every situation.

The third management issue concerns the way of handling individual relationships. Evidently, the interaction process, and its connections with other relationships, have to be effectively managed in order to make the relationship productive from a technological and commercial point of view. There are several related questions. First of all, what should the relationship be used for? For example, should the cooperation be restricted to a single project limited in time and scope or should it be part of a broader and more long-term cooperative relationship? To what extent should the cooperation be formalized through the signing of written contracts or the establishment of a joint organization? How should the technological results be exploited? For example, how should the proprietary rights be divided between the parties?

It should be emphasized that the problem of managing an individual relationship is not only related to the two interacting parties and the exchange between them. As both actors have other relationships part of the problem has to do with the connections with these relationships. As explained in the previous description of the interaction model, individual relationships should always be seen and managed in a network context.

The issues and questions raised here are relevant for managers. At the same time they also constitute important research topics. Many of the interaction and network studies referred to above deal with these questions and have in different ways contributed to shed light on them.[4] The present study gives an opportunity to explore the three identified management and research issues further. In the analysis of the two cases we shall therefore come back to some of the questions discussed here.

Chapter 3

Methodology

The basic design of the project was to carry out a limited number of in-depth case studies. Given the previously described framework and research questions, the cases to be selected should be concerned with the development of industrial goods and assumingly be of interest from an interaction and network point of view. In other words, there should be a known element of external technological cooperation. This means, of course, that the cases are not necessarily representative of 'the Japanese way of developing new industrial products', if there happens to be any such model.[1] But given the assumption that buyer–seller interaction is of fundamental importance to technological development, it can anyway be expected that such a study would contribute at least some valuable new insights into the field of industrial innovation. Although the study should have it own merits, of course, it is important to note that it belongs to a broader stream of research on industrial networks to which it can be related.

It was decided to look for cases in the area of advanced structural materials – in the first instance, fine ceramics and steel. The main reason for this was the possibility to relate the results to other studies of the same industries that had been, or were planned to be, carried out in Sweden. After some search for suitable study objects it was finally decided to concentrate the research on two particular cases. One is concerned with Toshiba Corporation and its development and commercialization of silicon nitride ceramics. Silicon nitride is one of the new advanced ceramic materials which is being developed around the world for high-temperature structural applications. Although the real breakthrough in the marketplace has not taken place yet Toshiba can be seen to be one of the leading manufacturers of this material. Over the past ten years Toshiba's development of silicon nitride products has to a large extent been carried out in close cooperation with an American customer, Cummins Engine Company.

The other case deals with Nippon Steel Corporation and the development of corrosion-resistant steel for the automobile industry. More specifically, the case focuses on the development and commercialization of one specific product; namely, two-layered zinc–iron coated steel sheet for autobodies. This product was developed in the early 1980s together with Toyota Motor Corporation.

The writing of the cases was based primarily on interviews with a limited number of senior managers and researchers in Toshiba and Nippon Steel who had played key roles in the investigated projects. Some useful data were also obtained through more informal discussions with other people. In the case of Toshiba, interviews were also carried out in the United States with key representatives of Toshiba's principal partner, Cummins Engine, and of Enceratec (a US-based joint venture between Toshiba and Cummins). It would have been desirable to have conducted interviews with Toyota as well, but unfortunately this was not possible mainly because the key persons involved in the project were not available.

In parallel with the study of Toshiba's silicon nitride project a separate study was carried out with the purpose of providing a broad overview of the development of fine ceramics in Japan (Laage-Hellman, 1991). The data were collected by reviewing the literature on this topic available in English and, above all, by interviewing representatives of several Japanese governmental agencies, trade associations, and research organizations. Some of the information obtained in these interviews has been used in writing the Toshiba case.

On the basis of the early interviews, drafts of the cases were written and sent to the companies. After that new interviews were carried out in order to collect complementary data and correct misunderstandings. This procedure was repeated several times. In this way the cases gradually emerged and finally took the form they have in the present book. For the reason of confidentiality certain parts of the earlier versions have been omitted or rewritten after requests from the companies.

The ambition was to write cases that covered the entire story from the very beginning up till the fall of 1992 (the point in time in which the data collection was finished and the companies gave their permission to publish the cases). In accordance with the interaction and network approach, though, the main focus is on the interplay of the two focal companies with various external units (rather than on the organization and management of the internal development work). The two relationships between Toshiba and Cummins and between Nippon Steel and Toyota, respectively, are described in as much detail as possible, given the data that could be collected and disclosed. In line with the network perspective, other actors and relationships of importance for the understanding of the focal relationships were also identified. However, it has not been possible to examine these relationships as thoroughly as the focal ones.

Besides the interaction with external parties, the internal interplay within the companies has been described to some extent. This interplay is of importance, especially in the Toshiba case where several companies/organizational units within the Toshiba and Cummins groups have been involved.

The three management issues identified toward the end of the preceding chapter constitute the starting point for the analysis (Chapter 6). In the reasoning some of the observed phenomena have been related to what has been learnt from other studies. By drawing on previous research it has been possible to use the cases more efficiently to illustrate general network problems and to discuss more generally applicable implications. In other words, the arguments put forward in this chapter are not exclusively based on the two Japanese cases but also on knowledge and insights gained through other studies.

Chapter 4

Development and commercialization of Zn–Fe alloy coated steel sheet for autobodies
The case of Nippon Steel

4.1 INTRODUCTION

In May 1983 DUREXCELITE, a new type of corrosion-resistant steel sheet produced by Nippon Steel Corporation (NSC) was introduced in the commercial production of automobile bodies at Toyota Motor Corporation. The new steel was the result of a three-year intensive development cooperation between Nippon Steel and Toyota. The introduction of DUREXCELITE meant that Toyota could take a new major step in improving the protection of auto-bodies against corrosion and that Nippon Steel could strengthen its position as the number one supplier of auto sheet material to Toyota, the largest automobile manufacturer in Japan.

This case focuses on the interaction between Nippon Steel and the Japanese automobile makers, in particular Toyota, in the development of DUREXCELITE and other types of surface-treated steel sheet for automotive use.

4.2 NIPPON STEEL CORPORATION

Nippon Steel is the world's largest steelmaker with about a 30 percent domestic share in crude steel production. Its manufacturing program covers all kinds of ordinary steel products including wire rod, plates, hot- and cold-rolled sheet and pipes, as well as stainless and other specialty steels. In fiscal year 1990 (April 1990 to March 1991) Nippon Steel produced 29 million tons of crude steel and had a total turnover of 2.6 trillion yen. Approximately 80 percent of sales came from the steel sector. More than 15 percent of steel production was exported. At the end of that same year the number of employees amounted to 54,000 (38,200 in the parent company and 15,800 in subsidiaries).

History

It was in 1970 that Nippon Steel was formed by a merger of Yawata Iron & Steel Co. and Fuji Iron & Steel Co. However, the original founding of what is now Nippon Steel dates back to 1857 when Japan's first modern blast furnace went into operation at Kamaishi, and to 1901 when the government-operated Yawata Steel Works was inaugurated. In 1979 the company got its present organization structure which consists of five sub-organizations of head office, steelworks, corporate organization (including R&D), engineering, and new business.

The modern Nippon Steel, with its ten steelworks, has since its foundation not only been the world's largest steel firm but a technological leader as well. Over the past twenty years a great number of internationally recognized R&D achievements in steelmaking have been made by Nippon Steel.

During the 1970s and 1980s, however, Nippon Steel, like the other large integrated steelmakers in Japan, has been severely affected by unfavorable market conditions and increasing competition from domestic and foreign steelmakers. This has forced the company to adjust its production capacity and to branch out into new fields of business. In 1984 Nippon Steel announced a major rationalization plan according to which the company would concentrate its integrated iron and steel operations into four efficient works – Kimitsu, Oita, Yawata, and Nagoya – and renovate the other plants for specialty production.

In addition to this rationalization plan Nippon Steel continued to diversify aggressively into technologically related fields with the aim of becoming a 'total basic materials producer'. As a complement to existing businesses in nonferroalloys, chemicals, construction, and plant engineering Nippon Steel started new projects in such areas as titanium, fine ceramics, electronics, information systems, biotechnology, and urban redevelopment. In 1987, following a year of heavy losses, Nippon Steel launched a new medium- and long-term plan for 'multiple-business management'. It stated that steelmaking and new business areas with high growth potential were the two main centers of interest. As to steel, the plan contained elements of continued regrouping and relocation of production facilities, reduction of the workforce, updating and expansion of facilities for products in strong demand, and development of new products. These efforts were aimed at maintaining the company's international competitiveness. Despite the rapid expansion into new fields, steelmaking would thus remain the core business of Nippon Steel. The target of the long-range plan was, and still is, that steel should account for 60 percent of the company's 4,000 billion yen sales in the late 1990s. Moreover, the philosophy behind the diversification strategy was that all new businesses should be related to steelmaking or other technologies already accumulated within the company.

Research and development

R&D related to the steel business is carried out within the Technical Development Bureau, which belongs to the Corporate Organization. The Technical Development Bureau was established in 1991 and includes four corporate and nine steelworks-based laboratories (Figure 4.1). It has a total staff of approximately 2,800 persons (1,100 researchers, 400 plant engineers, 1,000 technicians, and 300 in management and administration).

The Steel Research Laboratories, with a mission 'to create new steel products for customers (e.g., coated steel sheet) and to develop new production processes for next decade,' have their origin within Fuji Iron & Steel's central research organization established in 1959. They now constitute one of the four corporate R&D units and since 1991 have been located in Futtsu City (Chiba Prefecture) where Nippon Steel has constructed a new Research & Engineering Center. This center is situated close to the Kimitsu Works and will integrate all functions of the company's research, development, and engineering activities.

In line with the overall corporate goal to achieve the strongest possible competitiveness in the steel business, the aim of the Steel Research Laboratories is to develop new products (including software):

- for identified strategic market sectors, such as automobiles, energy, and shipbuilding among others,
- with ultimate properties (strength, toughness, ductility, corrosion resistance, etc.),
- with new functions (e.g., noise reduction), and
- with high reliability.

The aim is also to modify existing manufacturing processes and to develop new ones in order to reduce costs and create new

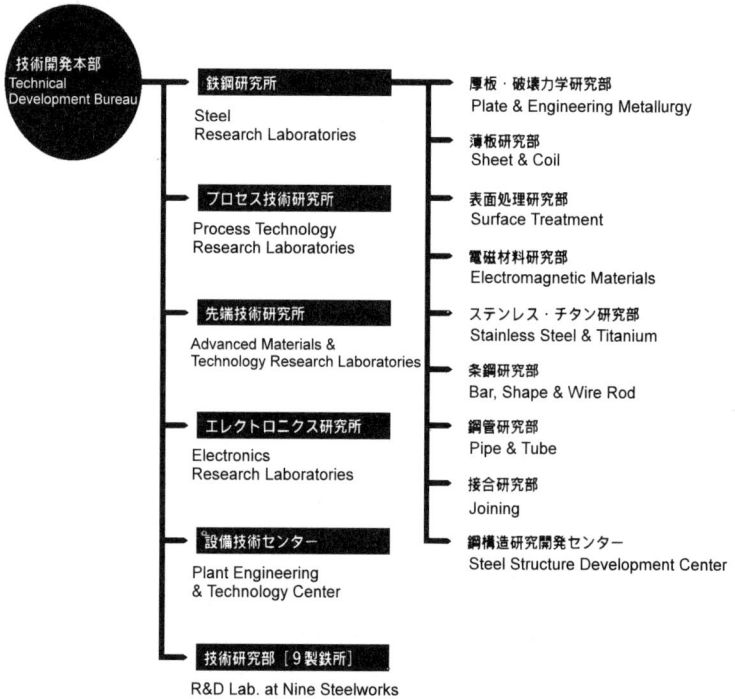

技術開発本部
Technical
Development Bureau

鉄鋼研究所
Steel
Research Laboratories

厚板・破壊力学研究部
Plate & Engineering Metallurgy

薄板研究部
Sheet & Coil

プロセス技術研究所
Process Technology
Research Laboratories

表面処理研究部
Surface Treatment

電磁材料研究部
Electromagnetic Materials

先端技術研究所
Advanced Materials &
Technology Research Laboratories

ステンレス・チタン研究部
Stainless Steel & Titanium

条鋼研究部
Bar, Shape & Wire Rod

エレクトロニクス研究所
Electronics
Research Laboratories

鋼管研究部
Pipe & Tube

接合研究部
Joining

設備技術センター
Plant Engineering
& Technology Center

鋼構造研究開発センター
Steel Structure Development Center

技術研究部 [9製鉄所]
R&D Lab. at Nine Steelworks

Figure 4.1 The organization of the Technical Development Bureau
Source: Nippon Steel Corporation

properties. Another important task is to clarify to users the advantages of steel compared to other materials or solutions.

As shown in Figure 4.1, the Steel Research Laboratories consist of nine different laboratories. In 1991 they employed 210 researchers altogether. The corresponding number of researchers working in the same fields at the steelworks was 220. Mr Kametaro Itoh, Director of the Steel Research Laboratories, says that this ratio, close to 1:1, is ideal for promoting R&D activities in a company like Nippon Steel.

The activities of each laboratory are focused on a certain product area and cover not only basic research but also new products, production processes and application technologies such as quality evaluation and utilization processes. In addition, the Steel Research Laboratories serve as a central research body for fundamental technologies such as fracture, machinability, press formability, vibration damping, rust prevention, adhesion, heat resistance, corrosion resistance, welding and joint technology.

An important element in the policy of the Steel Research Laboratories is to strengthen research cooperation with internal as well as external parties. Internally, it is considered important to have a close and well-functioning cooperation – especially with the plant engineering division and the works-based R&D laboratories. Externally, the customers constitute the most important category of partners. Approximately 70 percent of all external R&D cooperation is related to customers.

In some cases these customer cooperations take place within the frame of a company-wide, permanent joint R&D organization. From the end of the 1970s, Nippon Steel has taken the initiative to establish such organizations at the corporate level with several of its largest domestic customers. Typically, the joint organization consists of a chairman (vice-president level), a steering committee (director level), and a number of R&D groups for different types of steel products (plate, sheet, bar, tube, etc.). These groups are permanent and normally meet twice a year to exchange information and discuss technical questions of common interest. When needed temporal subgroups are formed in order to work on specific tasks, such as the development of a new product or application.

Today Nippon Steel has this kind of long-term cooperative agreement with about ten of its largest customers in Japan. The experiences are very good. Several important product innovations have, for example, been produced in this way. The NSC people think that this kind of relationship between steelmaker and steel user is unique for Japan. No other domestic competitor has the same kind of broad cooperation with its customers.

Nippon Steel also engages in joint research and development activities with universities, both in Japan and abroad, and with suppliers of manufacturing equipment. Mitsubishi Heavy Industries, Kawasaki Heavy Industries and Hitachi are examples of important machinery suppliers with which Nippon Steel is developing new process technology. Furthermore, together with other Japanese steelmakers Nippon Steel participates in several national programs coordinated and supported by the Ministry of International Trade and Industry (MITI) or the Science and Technology Agency (STA).

Joint research and development with customers and other internal or external parties is thus considered to be an important success

factor for the Steel Research Laboratories. Mr Itoh mentions some
other factors that he believes to be essential in promoting the
technological development:

- competition with time (i.e., shortening the lead-time in product
  development),
- direction of basic research toward specific targets (the researchers often have their own 'hobbies' which they would doubtless
  pursue were it not for management directing them toward specific targets),
- a global approach,
- measures for the generation of rapid change,
- motivation of the younger generation in order to secure recruit-
  ment, and
- fair appreciation and evaluation of each group and person.

4.3 DEVELOPMENT OF COATED STEEL SHEET FOR AUTOMOTIVE BODIES: HISTORICAL BACKGROUND

Zinc and tin coating has been used in industry to protect steel sheet
against corrosion for a very long time. Important application areas
have been containers (e.g., food cans), construction, electric machine and household appliances, and automobiles. During the past
10–15 years the consumption of these so-called corrosion-resistant
steel sheets has increased rapidly, especially in the automotive field,
along with the development and commercial introduction of a
range of new, more sophisticated and effective protective coatings,
most of which are based on some kind of zinc alloy. In 1989 the
Japanese market for coated steel sheet amounted to 12 million tons.
Of this tonnage, 35 percent went to the automotive industry; this
compares with 15 percent ten years earlier. As to Nippon Steel, 44
percent of its 3.7 million tons of coated steel produced in the same
year was intended for automotive use.

Since the early 1970s corrosion protection, particularly of the
autobody, has been an important topic in the automobile industry. The reason is that the lifespan of the automobile is becoming longer. Corrosion of the autobody had become a serious
problem, especially in cold climatic areas such as North America
and Northern Europe where de-icing agents were used in large
quantities.

Corrosion of the autobody, proceeding in the presence of water and oxygen and with chloride ion prominently accelerating the rate, can be categorized into two major types – namely, perforative and cosmetic. *Perforative corrosion* is caused by the accumulation of dust, water and salt on the bottom of an automobile's box structure. It proceeds from the inside to the outside and results in perforation. *Cosmetic corrosion*, in the form of damaged paint portions on the outer surface, is caused by, for example, stone fragments hitting the automobile. It spreads parallel to the surface and deteriorates its appearance.

The two categories of corrosion thus have different proceeding mechanisms and therefore require different preventive methods. There are four principal protection techniques used in various combinations by the automakers (Figure 4.2):

1 The automobile design, e.g. improvements in structure to prevent accumulation of water and to expedite the flow of various fluids.
2 The painting system, e.g. full-dip phosphating and primer coating.
3 The use of partial rust prevention such as edge sealer, adhesives, and chipping primer.
4 The use of corrosion-resistant steel.

It is up to each automaker to decide which of these four methods should be concentrated on and how to combine them in designing the corrosion-resistant system. Differences in the use of corrosion-resistant steel among countries and individual automobile manu-

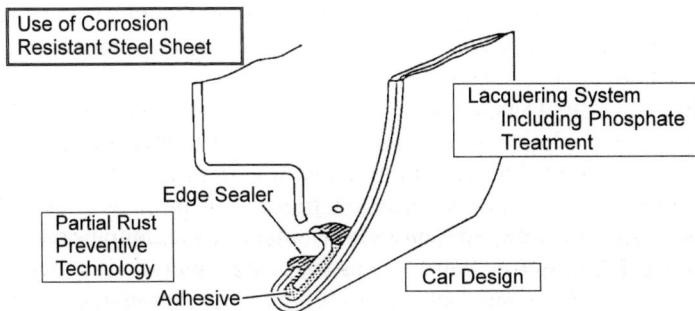

Figure 4.2 Protection methods against corrosion of automobile bodies
Source: Nippon Steel Corporation

facturers can thus be explained by the adoption of different concepts for corrosion protection (and the fact that the different methods affect each other).

The first use of coated steel sheet for autobodies took place in the United States in 1975, when the American automakers started to use Zincrometal (i.e., steel sheet coated with an organic material which contains zinc powder). This technology had been developed by Diamond Shamrock, a leading producer of organic paint, and introduced into the market by several US steelmakers.

In Japan, Toyota became the pioneer in introducing coated steel sheet. In 1977, two years after its American competitors, Toyota started to use so-called galvannealed steel supplied by Nippon Steel. This product was made through a hot-dip galvanizing process where the steel passes through an on-line heat treatment to diffuse the zinc into the steel surface and form a protective layer consisting of a Zn–Fe alloy with 88 percent Zn content (the term 'galvanized' is commonly used to denote steel sheet with a pure zinc layer). This coating technology had been introduced by Nippon Steel's Nagoya Works in the early 1960s based on a license from National Steel in the US. In the beginning Nippon Steel did not have any customers for this product, but after many efforts to find suitable applications a fruitful cooperation was finally established with Matsushita Electric, one of the largest producers of home appliances in Japan. Together they developed a steel sheet with thin coating layer (30 g/m^2) for electric washing machines (a thin layer was desired in order to achieve a good formability and weldability). The good quality of the new corrosion-resistant steel, leading to longer life of the products, was at the time used by Matsushita as an important sales argument– for example when advertising the new machines on television.

In 1977 the technical service people of Nippon Steel suggested that Toyota use hot-dip galvannealed steel sheet, marketed under the tradename of DURGRIP, in its production of autobodies. This type of steel, exhibiting fairly balanced properties of corrosion resistance, press formability and weldability, was thought to be a good solution for Toyota, given the required durability of the autobody at that time. One reason for the suitability of this product was that Toyota and Matsushita shared the same kind of philosophy with regard to corrosion protection. For example, both of them measure the corrosion resistance of the steel after painting (there are others who aim at obtaining as good a corrosion resistance as is possible before painting).

While Matsushita used two-side coated steel sheet, Toyota wanted coating on the inner side only since there were some problems with the paintability. These problems were caused by cratering appearing when applying cathodic E-coat ('primer') on the coated surface (this cathodic electrodeposition, on both sides of the sheet, is done after phosphate treatment of the cold rolled surface and before painting on the outside). In order to produce one-side galvannealed steel sheet for Toyota, Nippon Steel first developed a special grinding method to remove the coating layer on one side. Later on Nippon Steel developed a technique which enabled them to make one-side coated steel sheet directly in the process line.

Since 1980 the galvannealed steel sheet for Toyota and other automotive customers has been produced in the new continuous hot-dip galvanizing line (CGL), which had been installed at Nagoya Works (Figure 4.3).

Mr Itoh strongly emphasizes the importance of the early development work on corrosion-resistant steel carried out together with Matsushita. The result of this work later on served as a starting point for the development of new products for the automotive industry.

4.4 THE CASE OF DUREXCELITE

The idea and project start

In spite of positive results achieved with DURGRIP, Toyota continued its efforts to improve the corrosion resistance of the autobody. Already toward the end of the 1970s it was clear that the existing one-side galvannealed steel could not adequately meet the increasing market demands. There were several problems.

One of them concerned the *press formability* (and weldability) of high-strength galvannealed steel. In order to save weight (and reduce fuel consumption) high-strength steel was increasingly applied to the outer body panels and other parts of the automobile body. However, due to the heating procedure the galvanizing process deteriorated the formability of the cold rolled steel, which in turn resulted in insufficient quality on some parts.

Another problem had to do with *cosmetic corrosion* on the outer panels when trying to use the coated surface for the outside of the

4HI- SPM

C- DSR   Plating Cell

ZAC- L

Galvannealing
Furnace

Cooler

▽FL + 53.5 m ----Top Roll

AJC

UCP post Treatment

POT

JCF

SCF

R   F

Strip temperature control

NOF

E- DSR

▽FL+21m

DURGRIP - E by electrolytic
plating cells

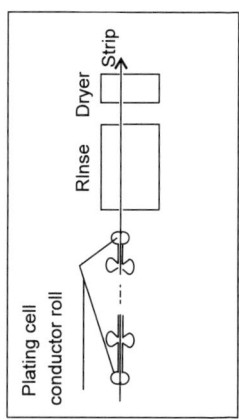

Strip

Rinse   Dryer

Plating cell
conductor roll

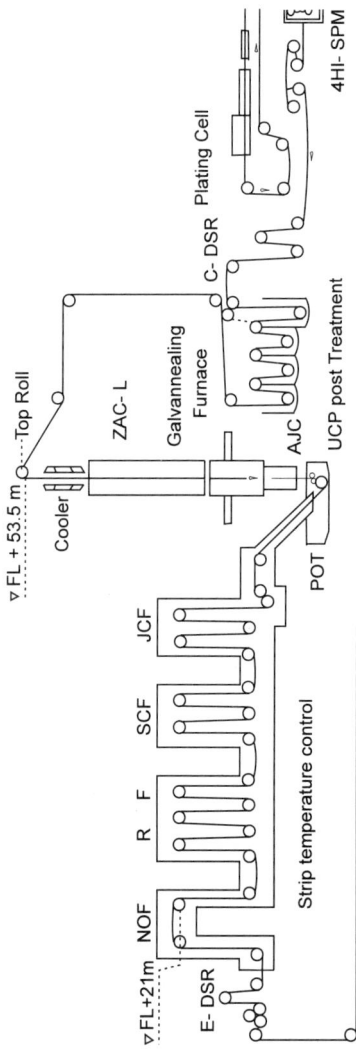

One side GI by the roll
coating process (UCP)

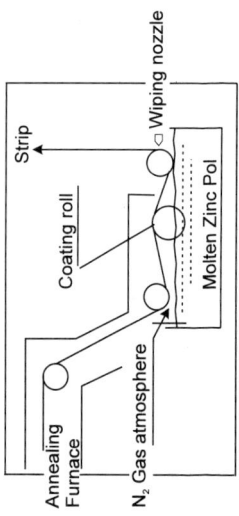

Strip

Wiping nozzle

Coating roll

Molten Zinc Pol

Annealing
Furnace

N_2 Gas atmosphere

Products

for the automotive use

1. Galvanneabed
2. One side Coated
3. One and a Half
4. DURGRIP- E

Specification

Capacity	31,000 ton/M
Thickness	0.4~1.6 mm
Width	610~1,585 mm
Center Speed	200 (Max) mpm
F' ce Capacity	57ton/Hr at 0.8X^{w}1585mm
Line Length	228 m
Operation	From 8 January 1979

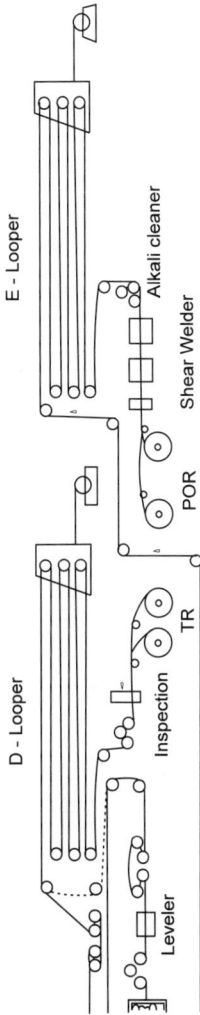

D - Looper E - Looper

Leveler

Inspection

TR

POR

Shear Welder

Alkali cleaner

Line Feature

1. All technical facilities for automotive use.
   a. One side coating machine (UCP)
   b. Electrolytic plating cell
   c. Heavy coat galvanneabed sheets producing techniques.
      (Zinc-Alloy Control by Laser intrgrated reflection, ZAC-L.)
2. All vertical furnace Incl. NOF.
3. One operator for material uncoiling and product coiling.
4. High accuracy strip temperature measuring system.

Figure 4.3 Continuous galvanizing line No. 4 at Nagoya Works
Source: Nippon Steel Corporation

LIQUID CUSHION CELL

LINE ARRANGEMENT

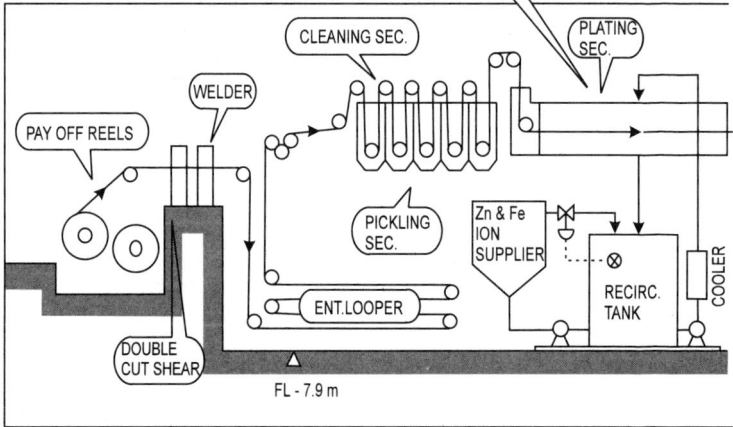

FL - 7.9 m

SPECIFICATION		
CAPACITY		34000 t/M
LINE SPEED		200 m/min
THICKNESS		0.4 – 1.6 mm
WIDTH		600 – 1,600 mm
COIL	ENTRY	42 t max. 508ϕ, 610ϕ I.D.
	DELIVERY	25 t max. 508ϕ, 610ϕ I.D.
NOS. OF PLATING CELL		8 CELLS
PLATING CURRENT		20 KA x 16 x 2
LOOPER	ENTRY	192 m, 6st
	DELIVERY	189 m, 6st
LINE LENGTH		181m

LAYOUT

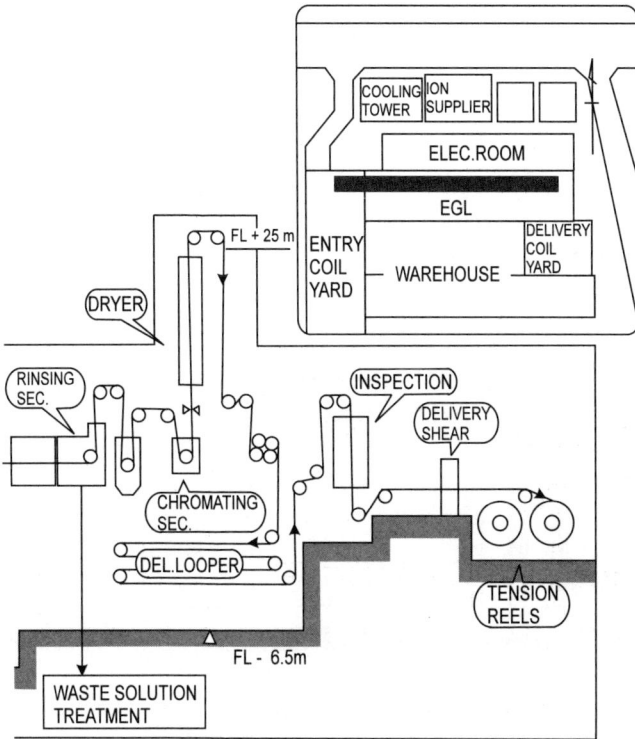

Figure 4.4 Electrolytic galvanizing line No.1 at Nagoya Works
Source: Nippon Steel Corporation

automobile body (which was desirable in order to improve the perforative corrosion resistance). The galvannealed steel tended to produce a rough surface made of small craterform paint film defects resulting from the cathodic electrodeposition of the primer.

Third, there was a desire to *reduce the coating weight* of the zinc layer as this would result in significant advantages to the automobile manufacturers (e.g., reduced flaking problems in the stamping operations, increased productivity in the coating line, and higher value of the recycled scrap).

These problems and needs were well known by the researchers at the R&D laboratory of Nippon Steel's Nagoya Works where the galvannealed steel sheet for Toyota was produced. At the end of 1979 one of the research engineers, Mr Tatsuya Kanamaru, came up with an idea for a new type of corrosion-resistant steel that would meet the requirements. Mr Kanamaru had long experience of developing coated steel sheet and had been involved already in the Matsushita project in the mid-1960s. One important part of his concept was to use the electroplating process (Figure 4.4), previously used only for pure Zn and Zn–Ni alloy coating, instead of hot-dip galvanizing. The former did not require any heating operation and therefore did not impair the formability of the base material. Furthermore, electroplating facilitated the attainment of a uniform thin layer and multiple layer coating. In order to use the coated surface on the outside without causing cosmetic corrosion Mr Kanamaru suggested the application of a very thin upper Fe-rich Zn–Fe layer on top of the Zn-rich Zn–Fe coating. Laboratory experiments had shown that a high Fe/Zn ratio layer gave an excellent surface finish by suppressing the cratering tendency during the cathodic electrodeposition of the primer, and in addition improved the paintability and the anti-creepage properties of the steel.

Mr Kanamaru had thus come up with a totally new concept of corrosion-resistant steel, *two-layered Zn–Fe electroplated steel sheet* (DUREXCELITE), which was thought to solve many of the corrosion problems found in the automotive industry.

To determine the chemical composition and coating weights of the two layers a series of small-scale tests were carried out by Mr Kanamaru and his co-workers, assisted by the central Surface Treatment Research Laboratory. Based on the results of this research it was tentatively concluded that the structure illustrated in Figure 4.5 should be optimal.

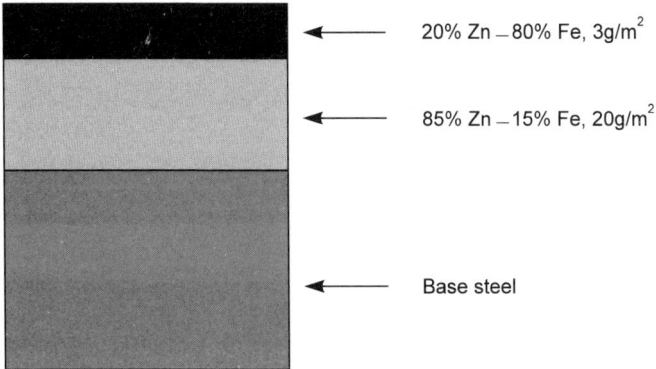

20% Zn – 80% Fe, $3g/m^2$

85% Zn – 15% Fe, $20g/m^2$

Base steel

Figure 4.5 Structure of two-layer Zn–Fe coating film
Source: Toda *et al.* (1984, p. 2)

Nippon Steel had already developed proprietary test methods to simulate the corrosion conditions in the automotive industry, but in order to develop a commercial product it would be necessary to evaluate the new coated steel through corrosion tests on actual autobodies. Nippon Steel thus needed a partner in the automotive industry. It was natural to approach Toyota for a number of reasons: first, it was Nagoya Works' largest customer of coated steel sheet for automotive use; second, an established technical cooperation already existed between the two companies. Also, the application of galvannealed steel sheet for autobodies had already been developed jointly by the two companies. Furthermore, the new product idea had come up in response to requirements and wishes expressed by Toyota in discussions between the two companies. In addition, Toyota was considered to be a reliable and technically competent user. Among other resources it had a large materials R&D department where a group of 5–6 engineers were working on coated steel sheet.

The development and testing phase

In the summer of 1980 the idea was introduced to Toyota. In spite of the limited experimental base available at this stage Toyota responded positively. As illustrated in Figure 4.6 preliminary evaluation of cut samples (150-mm width), made in a small pilot plant

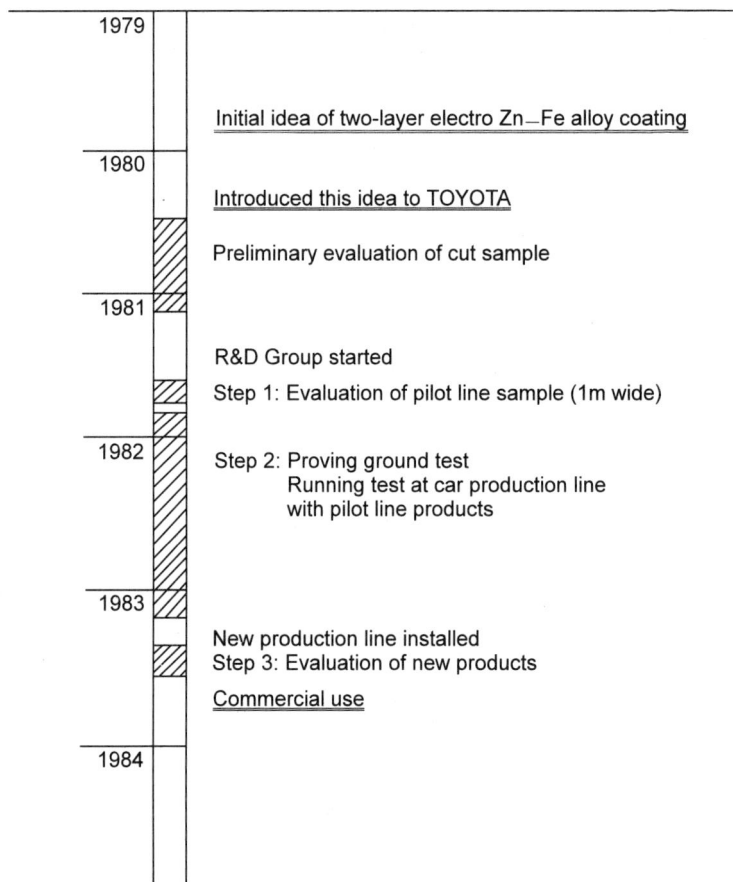

Figure 4.6 Different steps in developing DUREXCELITE

in Nagoya, was carried out by Toyota during the following seven months. One year later, in summer 1981, Nippon Steel and Toyota decided to establish a special joint R&D group to work on the project. The NSC team consisted of some fifteen people and was led by Mr Kametaro Itoh, who at this point in time was General Manager of the Nagoya Works' R&D Laboratory. The team also included members from the Surface Treatment Research Laboratory, Nagoya Works' cold rolling division and quality control department, and the corporate headquarters in Tokyo (the latter was responsible for arranging the meetings).

The Toyota team was headed by the Deputy General Manager for the Materials Research and Process Development Department. It was somewhat larger than Nippon Steel's team, 25–30 people, and included representatives of several plants and the following corporate functions: materials research, vehicle evaluation, body production, body engineering, and production engineering.

The whole group (i.e., 40–45 persons), met once a year during the period 1981–3, but there were two subgroups, one for R&D and one for production, which met more frequently. In addition there were a lot of informal contacts between the meetings among individual members of the group.

The first thing to do (Step 1 in Figure 4.6) was to make a more thorough evaluation of the press formability and welding properties. To do this a 1-meter wide steel sheet was needed. It was produced in a new pilot line, consisting of a plating cell, a pickling line and an electrolytic cleaning section, which was built at Nagoya Works' cold rolling mill for this specific purpose. The pilot line was run jointly by the R&D laboratory and the mill, which at this stage of the project collaborated closely with each other. The sheet was delivered to Toyota's department for Materials Research and Process Development, which carried out the testing.

The results of forming tests with actual panels showed that the formability was the same before and after coating and that there were no flaking problems. The weldability and the paintability also proved to be sufficient. To further evaluate the corrosion resistance, cyclic corrosion tests in the laboratory were carried out simultaneously by Nippon Steel and Toyota. These tests showed that the new steel was superior to galvanized steel and equal to galvannealed steel in spite of a thinner coating layer.

As it was clear from these laboratory tests that two-layered Zn–Fe alloy electroplated steel had very promising properties, it was decided jointly by the two companies to go ahead and evaluate the new coated steel through corrosion tests on actual autobodies. This is Step 2 in Figure 4.6. The first thing to do was to carry out 'proving ground tests', i.e., on-vehicle tests with a combination of various corrosion-accelerating conditions similar to those that automobiles are exposed to during practical use. The result was that every tested steel part showed good perforation resistance. Having completed these on-vehicle tests the next activity became to make 10,000 front fender panels on the production line. These parts were carefully checked at each stage, such as in the stamping shop, body assembly and paint shop.

Toward the end of 1982, after a few months' testing of the fender panels, some problems with the coated steel were discovered in one section of Toyota's production line. This problem was fed back to the Nippon Steel engineers who had to go back to the pilot line and study the coating process once again. Besides this problem, which was rapidly solved by modifying the manufacturing process, the two-layered Zn–Fe alloy electroplated steel evidenced good quality and confirmed the conclusions which had been drawn earlier. The original concept had thus proved to be correct, and in contrast to the usual case the large-scale evaluation did not lead to any major changes in the product specifications. This was 'a very lucky story' as one of the engineers described it.

Parallel to the product testing, carried out jointly by Toyota and Nippon Steel, the latter worked intensively on developing the electroplating process itself – for example, how to supply the Zn–Fe solution and control the pollution. In addition, a large number of process parameters had to be determined, such as composition of the plating solution, current density, relative velocity between the strip and the solution, and temperature at the time of deposition. All this development work was done without the direct involvement of the Toyota people.

Commercial introduction

In early 1983 Toyota made the formal decision to change from galvannealed steel to DUREXCELITE. By that time Nippon Steel was already in the process of installing a new electrolytic galvanizing line at Nagoya Works. Nippon Steel needed to increase its capacity to produce electroplated steel, mainly to satisfy the anticipated demand from Toyota, but the line would also be used for production of galvanized (pure zinc-coated) steel sheet for the home appliances industry. The investment decision had been made almost two years earlier (July 1981), i.e. at the beginning of Step 1 (see Figure 4.6). It was an early decision, but it was justified by the promising laboratory test results. These had made the management of Nippon Steel confident that the new product would become a commercial success.

In May 1983 the new line began large-scale production of DUREXCELITE. Evaluation of the steel (Step 3 in Figure 4.6) showed that it had the same excellent quality as had been obtained previously in the pilot plant.

The new steel was first applied by Toyota to Mark II, a new automobile model which was introduced into the market in that year. DUREXCELITE was then gradually introduced in every new model launched by Toyota during the following four years. By that time a complete substitution had taken place, since the model life cycle of Toyota, like other Japanese automobile makers, is four years. As pointed out by one NSC engineer this was a very rapid change compared with the long time it usually takes to introduce a new material in the automotive industry.

Joint agreement

During the development phase there was only a simple contract that regulated the terms of collaboration between Toyota and Nippon Steel. However, in 1983 before starting large-scale usage of the new product, a more comprehensive agreement on the exploitation of the research results was established. This was considered important by the NSC people as Toyota was Nippon Steel's largest customer and DUREXCELITE represented a major technological innovation with great commercial potential. The contract was preceded by negotiations between the two parties and resulted in a joint agreement specifying among other things how the rights to the research results should be divided between the two companies. One aspect concerned the conditions under which DUREXCELITE could be used by other customers (these conditions, which included some unique elements, cannot be disclosed here for the reason of confidentiality).

Another important issue covered by the formal contract concerned the possibility for Toyota to buy the new steel from other suppliers. It is Toyota's policy to have at least two suppliers of every component and material it purchases. To be able to pursue this policy Toyota demanded that Nippon Steel license the patent rights to other steelmakers in Japan. However, for 18 months Nippon Steel was allowed to be the sole supplier. In 1985 a first license was granted to Sumitomo Metal Industries. Shortly afterwards NKK, Kawasaki Steel and Kobe Steel followed suit. As a natural result Nippon Steel's share of Toyota's purchasing of coated steel sheet decreased. But Nippon Steel remained the main source of such steel and still accounts for 'a major portion' of

Toyota's consumption of coated steel (Toyota does not tell its suppliers how it divides the purchased volumes).

In spite of the strong rivalry among the Japanese steelmakers and the importance of technology as a means of competition, Nippon Steel has an open-minded attitude to technology sharing. The automobile industry consumes large quantities of steel, all of which cannot be supplied by Nippon Steel, partly because of the customers' need for security of delivery. As the leading steelmaker in Japan, Nippon Steel feels obliged to share technology with its domestic competitors, thereby satisfying the wishes of the buyers. But there is also a belief within Nippon Steel that competition is important in order to stimulate the market growth. Thus, by licensing new products to other Japanese steelmakers, the demand for these products will increase more rapidly than would otherwise be the case. For Nippon Steel it is better to get a smaller share of a rapidly growing market than having a monopoly position in a small and slowly growing market.

But this does not mean that the companies do not compete with technology. Mr Takashi Hada, General Manager of the Surface Treatment Research Laboratory, emphasizes the importance of keeping the know-how in-house and points out that there are quality differences among the steelmakers. In the case of coated steel sheet, the development of DUREXCELITE together with Toyota gave Nippon Steel a competitive advantage in the mid-1980s. The licensees have only been granted the patent rights as such, and there has been no transfer of production or product know-how. He says that the competitors have not yet caught up and that they are still 2–3 years behind.

Summary of the results

From a technical point of view the most important result of the DUREXCELITE project was that Nippon Steel overcame the difficulties in producing Zn–Fe coated steel sheet by the electroplating process. Commercially, this strengthened Nippon Steel's competitiveness as supplier of corrosion-resistant steel to the Japanese automobile industry, and in particular Toyota. This is reflected in the rapid increase in Nippon Steel's sales of coated steel sheet to the domestic automakers. From 1985 to 1990 the deliveries of such products soared from 0.94 million tons per year to 1.62 (i.e., an increase of 72 percent). As to other segments of the market, such as home appliances and construction, the commercial effects of DUREXCELITE have been negligible. The reason is that the product is too expensive for these customers.

To what extent DUREXCELITE has changed the distribution of market shares among the Japanese steelmakers is difficult to say. Generally speaking, it is difficult for a steel company to increase its domestic market share because of the intense competition in the Japanese market. For example, when one of the companies comes up with a new product the others immediately respond by developing and introducing their own similar varieties. This pattern of competition, typical of Japan, contributes to conserve the market positions.

As part of the performance appraisal system for R&D, Nippon Steel has an internal award system for particularly outstanding achievements in technology. It is called the President's Prize and is given to about twenty projects annually. In 1984 the DUREXCELITE project was one of the selected achievements.

The successful development of a two-layer Zn–Fe coated steel sheet for automotive use has also attracted attention externally. In 1985 Nippon Steel was granted the Mainichi Industrial Technology Award for its development of DUREXCELITE. This is a prestigious prize instituted by *Mainichi Shimbun*, one of the largest daily newspapers in Japan.

4.5 OTHER DEVELOPMENTS

Figure 4.7 summarizes the changes in the use of coated steel sheet in Japan. In the preceding section the story behind Toyota's substitution of two-layer Zn–Fe alloy electroplated steel sheet for hot-dip galvanized steel in 1983 has been described. But already in 1980 Nippon Steel had put electrogalvanized Zn–Ni alloy coating to practical use. The pioneering customer in this case was Mazda. In the same year Nissan started to use Zincrometal produced by NSC's subsidiary Tayo Seiko.

An interesting feature of the development of corrosion-resistant steel is that Nippon Steel has developed different types of coatings for different customers. This is because the automobile companies, as perceived by the researchers at Nippon Steel, have adopted varying philosophies with regard to corrosion protection of the autobody. According to Mr Hada, Nissan, for example, differs from Toyota in that they want to optimize the corrosion-resistance

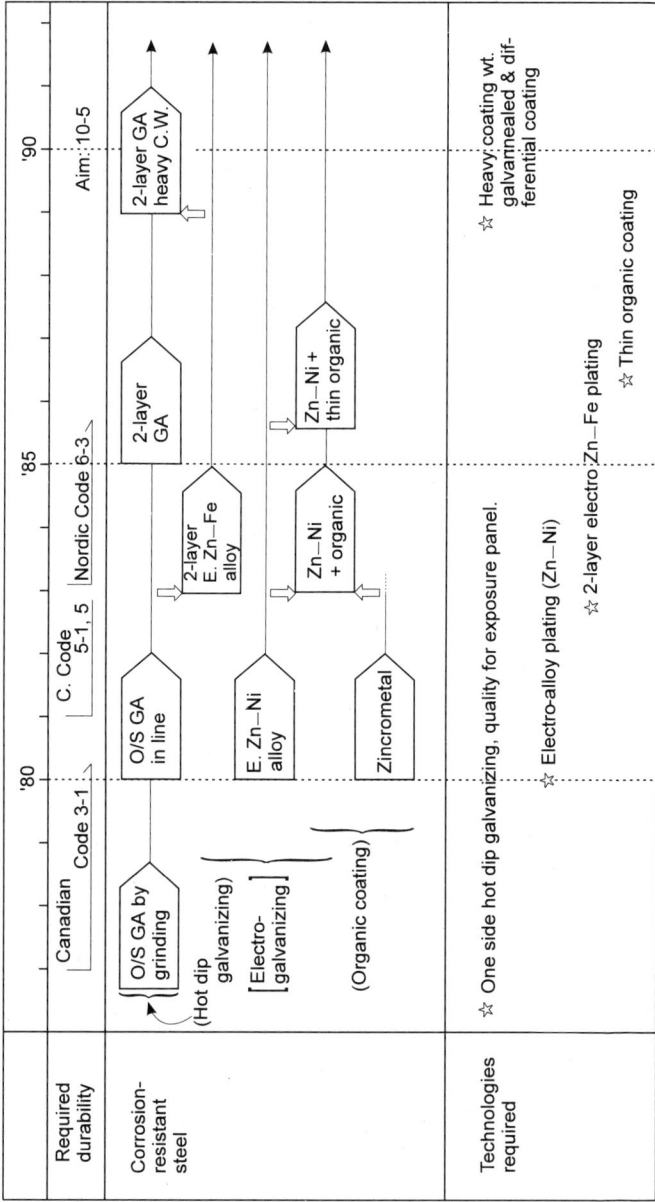

Figure 4.7 Changes in corrosion-resistant steel sheets for autobodies in Japan
Source: Hada (1989, p.113)

properties before painting (instead of after). They do not believe in painting certain portions and have chosen different structural designs compared to Toyota. This has driven them to go for other types of coating solutions. Together with Nissan, and to some extent in parallel to the development of DUREXCELITE, Nippon Steel has developed WELCOTE. It is a so-called organic composite coated steel sheet. The coating consists of a thin organic film on top of a Zn–Ni alloy layer. The development work was carried out in a similar way to that described above for DUREXCELITE. But in this case the product was made at Kimitsu Works, which is the main supplier to Nissan.

Mazda is another company which has switched over to WELCOTE. Honda's approach is perceived to be a little bit different. In contrast to other automobile manufacturers it uses several different types of coated steel and has its own evaluation methods.

It can be noted that Nippon Steel considers it to be an advantage, relative to its domestic competitors, to have four mills which can produce coated steel sheet. It makes it easier to handle the different customer relationships separately. Kawasaki Steel and NKK, for example, have only two mills, which forces them to mix production for different automakers. Nippon Steel not only separates the production but the development activities as well. There are separate teams working together with the different automakers. The contacts between these teams are purposely restricted in order to prevent confidential information about one customer being transmitted to other customers.

As indicated by Figure 4.7 the development of new coating technologies continued during the second half of the 1980s. The required durability of the automobiles has gradually increased and this has given incentives to steelmakers and automakers to continue their efforts to improve the corrosion resistance of the autobody. Thus Nippon Steel and Toyota have continued their collaboration. The work has centered on developing two-layer galvannealed steel with heavy coating weight ($60 \ g/m^2$). This is direction 2 indicated in Figure 4.8. But increasing the coating weight (with the purpose of improving the perforative corrosion resistance) requires the use of hot-dip galvanizing, since the electroplating process is too costly. To overcome the above-mentioned problem of poor weldability and formability of galvannealed steel, Nippon Steel has had to develop a new type of base material which can be processed at high temperatures without having its properties deteriorated. This

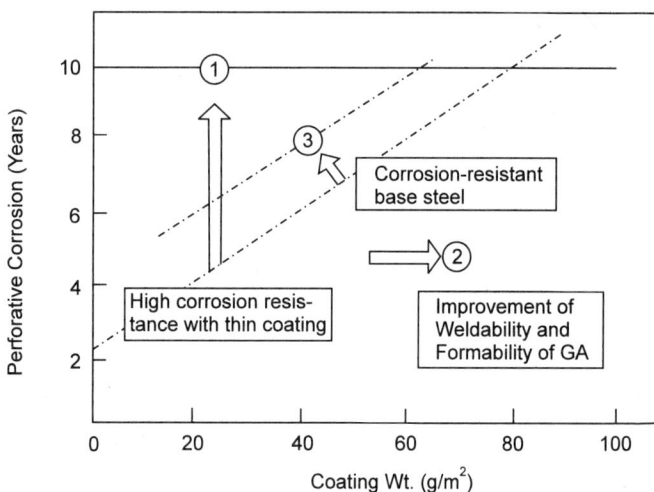

Figure 4.8 Targets of corrosion-resistant steel
Source: Nippon Steel Corporation

work was carried out independently by Nippon Steel and resulted in a new product for the automobile industry. DURGRIP-E, as the two-layer galvannealed steel sheet with heavy coating weight is called, has been offered to Toyota, who since 1990 has been once again in the process of changing steel. This time, however, the change is much easier as the structure and chemical composition of the coating film are the same as before.

Commenting on the differing concepts and coating technologies used by the Japanese automobile companies, Mr Hada says that it is too early to conclude which method gives the best corrosion resistance. It is only seven to eight years ago, he points out, since the automobile industry started to use the more advanced coating technologies to protect the autobody.

The aim is now to have ten-year durability against perforative corrosion and five-year against cosmetic corrosion. By using the diverse types of corrosion-resistant steel which have been introduced into the market since the early 1980s, the Japanese automotive industry has made great progress toward achieving this goal. However, the existing types of coated steel sheet do not entirely fulfill the required properties. The development efforts of auto-makers and steelmakers therefore continue. Having already learnt how to make high-strength steel sheet with heavy coating weight the main target of the current development activities is to achieve high corrosion resistance with thin coating weight (direction 1 in Figure 4.8).

4.6 INTERNATIONAL OUTLOOK

The development outside of Japan has been less straightforward. In Europe the picture is quite fragmented. The usage of coated steel sheet for the autobody began shortly after Japan (i.e., in the late 1970s) with Audi and Porsche as pioneers. Both used conventional hot-dip galvanized steel. In the case of Audi the steel was supplied by Thyssen, the leading manufacturer of coated steel in Europe. Since then a great deal of development efforts have been made by automobile manufacturers and steel suppliers and have resulted in the parallel usage of many different types of coatings and coating processes. However, the usage of galvannealed steel is still limited and there is so far no European manufacturer of two-layered steel sheet. Recently the trend has been influenced by Japanese auto-makers setting up an increasing number of transplants in Europe. This has spurred the interest in, for example, galvannealed steel and Zn–Ni electroplated steel. But so far none of the European produc-ers has tried to make Zn–Fe electroplated steel of the DUREX-CELITE type. This product is more difficult to make and requires technology that is not available in Europe.

The Japanese impact has been even stronger in the US, where the building of transplants began earlier than in Europe. In recent years several joint ventures have been established by Japanese and American steelmakers, and this has further contributed to increase the usage of typically 'Japanese coatings' such as galvan-nealed and Zn–Ni coated steel. Nippon Steel has a joint venture with Inland Steel to which the former's coating technology has been transferred. This mill will soon start supplying Toyota's two American plants with hot-dip two-layer galvannealed steel sheet with heavy coating weight. Up to now all coated autobody steel used by Toyota in the US has been imported from Japan.

According to representatives of Nippon Steel, the fact that the US has lagged behind Japan in the adoption of more advanced coating technologies can to a large extent be attributed to the traditionally poor relationships between American steelmakers and their customers in the automobile industry. This view is supported by the previously mentioned MIT study on the American industry, according to which the tenuous links between US steelmakers and auto producers have prevented the latter from optimizing the use of coated steel (Dertouzos *et al.*, 1989, p. 103). However, it seems that this situation has changed fairly dramatically during recent years (*Automotive Engineering*, 1991). Today all American steel producers seek to establish technological cooperation with the automotive companies. Like their Japanese counterparts both parties have recognized the advantage of early involvement of the steel supplier in the design and development of parts and their materials.

In Europe, the relationships between steelmakers and customers have traditionally been closer than in the US, and joint development of new steel products is nothing new. However, as pointed out by a representative of a European sheet producer, the R&D cooperation between steelmakers and automakers in Europe is probably not as extensive as it is in Japan. Neither is it institutionalized to the same degree.

4.7 SOME COMMENTS ON THE NIPPON STEEL CASE

This case is a good illustration of what can be achieved when a supplier and a customer are working closely together within an established long-term relationship. Although this project is considered by Nippon Steel to be an unusually successful example of joint development in terms of the technological and commercial results, it is not unique with regard to the role of the customer in the product development process. DUREXCELITE is only one in a row of coated steel sheet products which have been developed together with domestic customers during the last fifteen years. Nippon Steel has developed other types of coatings, not only with Toyota but with other automakers as well. In fact, Nippon Steel has for many years had a continual technological exchange with several of the major automobile manufacturers in Japan. However, it seems that the relationships with Toyota and Nissan, the two largest producers, have been the most extensive and the broadest in scope.

It can be argued that the development process described in this case is quite typical of how new steel products are developed and introduced into the market. The interplay between Nippon Steel and its large automotive customers in the domestic market is in many respects similar to the kind of patterns that have been found in earlier studies of the steel and other heavy industries (see, e.g., Laage-Hellman, 1984; Håkansson, 1987a). There are certainly differences, but these pertain more to how the exchange is carried out than to the basic role of customers in the innovation process.

The importance of long-term development cooperation between steelmakers and large customers was a striking finding in the previous studies. In spite of the strong export orientation of the Swedish steel industry the main partners were often domestic customers. Sometimes these relationships were several decades old. For example, the Nordic pulp and paper companies and their equipment suppliers played a historically important role for the development of the Swedish stainless steel industry in the 1950s and 1960s and still enjoy close relationships with their steel suppliers. But there are also examples of close technological cooperation with foreign customers. In one case, a specialty steel producer had collaborated continuously for more than ten years with an American customer. As a matter of fact, the product development in that application area (one of the most important to the company) had to a large extent been directed at satisfying the needs and wishes of that particular customer – one of the company's largest and technically most qualified. This approach proved to be successful and contributed to give the Swedish steelmaker a leading position in the world market for that product.

One thing which distinguishes the present case from the findings of the Swedish studies is the width of Nippon Steel's technological cooperation with its main domestic customers and the extent to which these relationships are institutionalized. Even though they were often long-lasting and close, the Swedish steelmakers' cooperative relationships with customers (domestic or foreign) were often informal in nature and based to a large extent on mutual trust and personal ties. Written contracts and formalized project organizations were not extensively used. No examples of permanent joint R&D groups of the type established by Nippon Steel were found. But as already mentioned this type of organization also seems to be rare in Japan.

Another interesting observation is the more or less parallel development of different products for different customers. For example, Nissan and Toyota, the two main rivals in the Japanese automobile market, use different approaches to corrosion protection, and this makes it necessary for Nippon Steel to provide separate solutions for these customers. What is nicely illustrated by this is the effect of the heterogeneity of resources, which as explained in the theory chapter is a fundamental characteristic of industrial networks. The existence of this heterogeneity on the buying side makes it difficult for the supplier to standardize the exchange that takes place with various customers.

Another common problem illustrated by the case has to do with the commercialization of the technology that comes out of the cooperation. There are natural and inherent conflicting interests between the parties that need to be handled within the relationship. This is an issue that will be dealt with in more detail in Chapter 6.

Finally, the Nippon Steel case offers a good illustration of inter-dependencies among different changes in a network. One of the main factors which initiated the development of DUREXCELITE was the auto industry's increasing use of high-strength steel (which in turn was the result of the rising oil price and the end-users' demand for automobiles with lower fuel consumption). But the introduction of high-strength steel created problems in the manu-facturing of coated steel sheet for autobodies and initiated the search for new coating technology. In the case of Toyota the result was that electroplating was substituted for hot-dip galvanizing. Later on, the steadily increasing demands on the corrosion resis-tance made it desirable to increase the thickness of the coating, and this necessitated a return to the hot-dip galvanizing process. In order to make that change possible a new product development activity had to be started. As a result, it gave a new type of high-strength steel which could be coated by hot-dip galvanizing.

What we have also seen here is an example of the varying value of a specific resource. As here it can be a certain process technol-ogy, but it can also be a certain piece of knowledge. Such a resource, which during one period of time becomes less valuable due to changes in the network, may later on regain value as a result of new developments. This phenomenon is typical of industrial networks and has obvious management implications. It is thus important to keep in mind that a certain resource, which at one particular point in time has lost its value, might possibly become useful again through combination with a new resource. Therefore, one should think twice before the resource is disposed of. Rather than divesting, it might be better to keep it and maintain it, even if this is associated with some costs.[1]

Chapter 5

Development and commercialization of structural fine ceramics
The case of Toshiba

5.1 INTRODUCTION

This case is concerned with Toshiba Corporation's development of silicon nitride ceramics for structural applications. 'Fine ceramics',[1] which besides silicon nitride comprises a number of other 'modern' ceramic materials such as alumina, silicon carbide and zirconia, is one of those so-called new materials which are subject to intensive research and development efforts in the advanced industrialized countries, notably Japan, the United States, Germany, Great Britain, and France.

Toshiba is one of the leading manufacturers of fine ceramics in Japan and has ever since the 1960s invested a lot of R&D resources in development of nitride ceramics for structural use. The case describes the entire research and development process, from the perspective of Toshiba, but focuses primarily on the development of diesel engine components during the 1980s. This development has to a large extent taken place in close cooperation with a US customer and partner, Cummins Engine Company.

5.2 FINE CERAMICS: DEFINITION AND CHARACTERISTICS

The Japanese Ministry of International Trade and Industry (MITI) defines fine ceramics in the following way:

> those inorganic materials which are characterized by a fine structure composed of numerous crystal particles, which are produced with manufacturing processes best suited for their intended applications by utilizing refined and adjusted chemical compositions to control the fine texture and form, so that the

specific selected functions inherent in the ceramics can be drawn out in full.

(Ishiguro, 1991, pp. 49–51)

Fine ceramics differs from 'classic ceramics' (such as pottery, glass and refractories) in that it is a high-technology material used for advanced industrial applications where tough demands are made on the performance of the material. Commonly, fine ceramics is divided into two main categories: functional ceramics and structural ceramics. The former are used because of their specific electromagnetic, optical or biological properties and find applications in such products as, for example, electronic tubes, semiconductor parts, electronic components, optical fibers, and medical implants. The structural ceramics are characterized by their excellent mechanical and thermal properties, especially high resistance to heat, wear and corrosion. Typical application areas are cutting tools, wear parts, bearings and engine components.

In terms of chemical composition the most common ceramic substances are alumina (Al_2O_3), silicon carbide (SiC), silicon nitride (Si_3N_4), aluminum nitride (AlN), and zirconia (ZrO_2). In addition there are 'alloys' and composite materials made up of various combinations of these and other substances.

The functional properties of fine ceramics have already brought about large scale use of such materials in the electronics and electrical industry. The scope of application is now being extended to structural materials that make the most of ceramics' high-temperature strength, corrosion resistance and abrasion resistance.

The weakness of fine ceramics as a structural material, compared with metals for example, is its 'brittleness'. This is due to the atomic structure of ceramics which does not allow the free movement of atoms and ions in solid states. This makes ceramics stable in nature and characterized by high resistance to heat and deformation. But for the same reason ceramics has low ductility and therefore is particularly susceptible to sudden fracture damage due to concentrated stress. A fine precise crystal structure and high cleanliness is therefore one of the keys to making a high-quality material and eliminating the poor reliability of fine ceramics which has been a major problem inhibiting its wider usage in structural applications.

Fine ceramics is produced through a complicated manufacturing process where powdered raw materials are formed, pressed and sintered into a finished product (see Figure 5.1 for a schematic

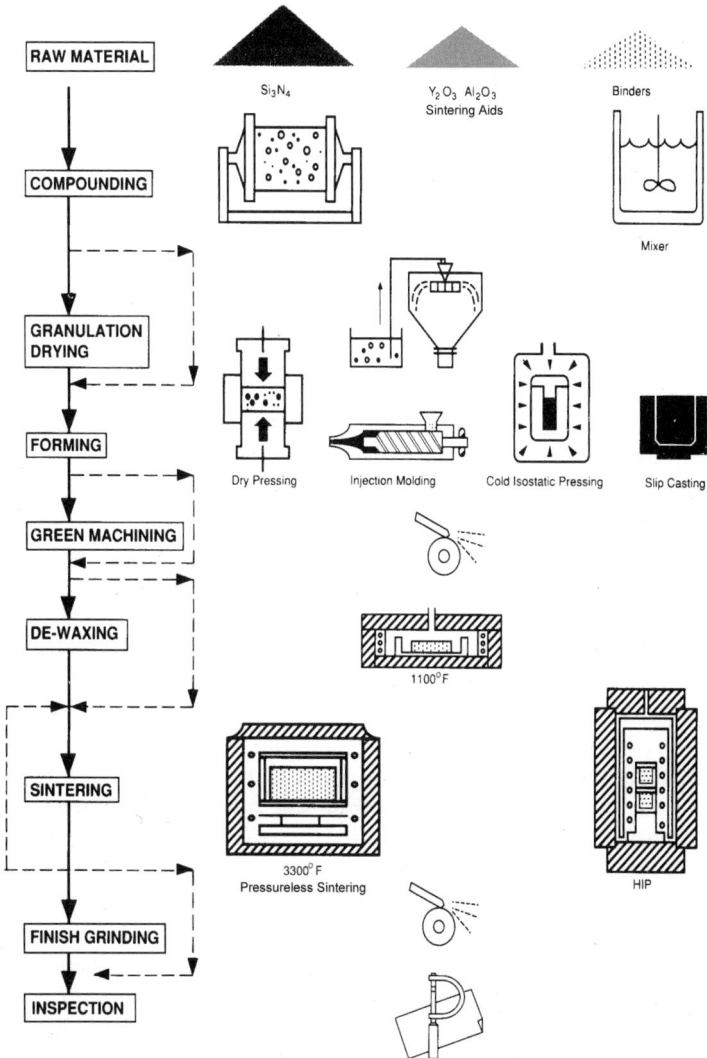

Figure 5.1 Manufacturing process for fine ceramics
Source: Enceratec

illustration of the process). Much of the R&D efforts aiming at developing fine ceramics for structural applications have centered on the quality and size of the powder and the development of new and more effective forming and heat processing methods in order to increase toughness. Since conventional design principles used for metals are not applicable to ceramics, large efforts are also made to develop new design methods which take into consideration the specific properties (e.g., the brittleness) of fine ceramics.

5.3 TOSHIBA

Toshiba Corporation, established in 1875, is one of the ten largest manufacturers of electronic and electrical goods in the world. In the fiscal year of 1990 (April 1990 to March 1991) Toshiba had 162,000 employees and achieved a turnover of 4,695 billion yen and a net income of 121 billion yen.

Besides its four main business areas – Information and Communication Systems, Electronic Devices, Heavy Electrical Apparatus, and Consumer Products – Toshiba also produces a wide range of other products and materials mainly for industrial applications. Since 1987 all materials-related business activities have been assembled within the Material & Components Group (Figure 5.2). However, Toshiba's involvement in the field of advanced materials is much older than that. In 1909, for example, Toshiba was the first Japanese company to produce tungsten wire for lamp filaments.

As is shown in Figure 5.2, the Material & Components Group consists of three internal divisions within the parent company and seven wholly or partly owned subsidiaries. Besides the Fine Ceramics Division two of the subsidiaries – namely, Toshiba Ceramics and Toshiba Tungaloy – are running ceramic businesses.

Toshiba Ceramics, with a turnover of 59 billion yen in fiscal year 1990, produces an extensive range of materials including silicon wafers for semiconductor manufacture, quartz and silica glass products, refractories for the iron and steel industry, and advanced ceramics. As to the latter, Toshiba Ceramics' silicon carbide, silicon nitride, alumina, and zirconia products are used in such applications as abrasion-resistant parts, furnace tubes, burner nozzles, and consumer products (e.g., knives, scissors and kitchen cleavers).

Toshiba Tungaloy is one of the leading Japanese manufacturers of cemented carbide cutting tools and wear parts. The 1990 net sales amounted to 45 billion yen. In 1958 Toshiba Tungaloy introduced the first alumina ceramic cutting tool in Japan. Since then several new ceramic products have been introduced into the

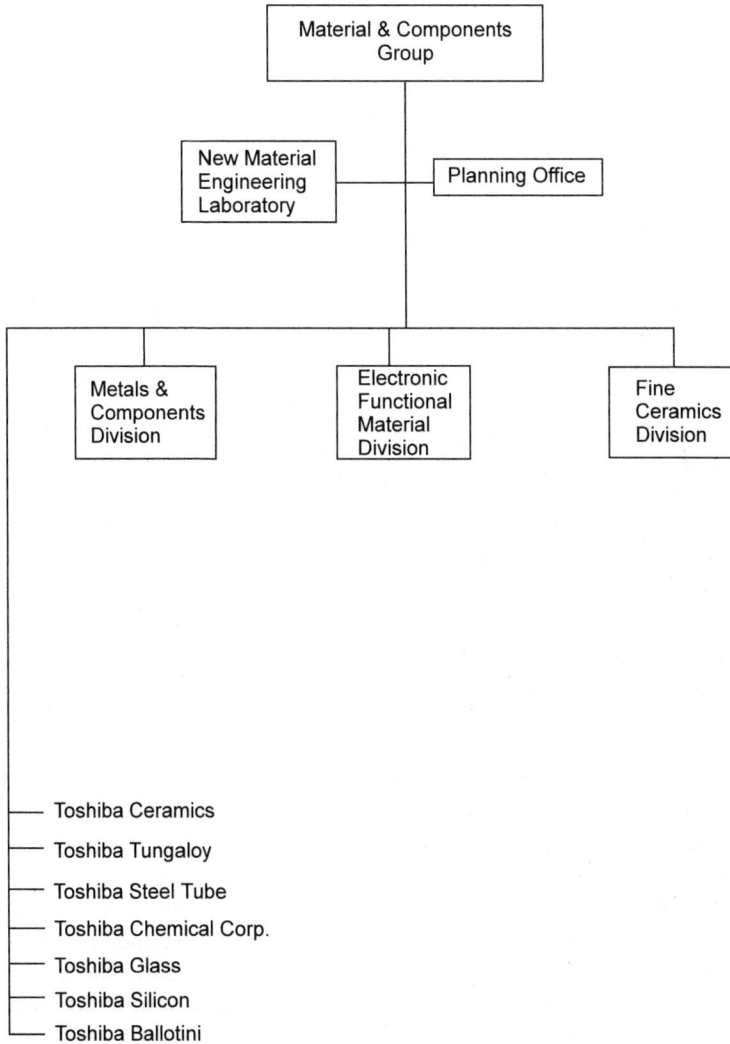

Figure 5.2 Organization of the Material & Components Group, Toshiba

market. These include silicon nitride grades for high-speed cutting, wear- and impact-resistant tools, and high-pressure sintered boron nitride grades for cutting difficult-to-machine materials. The manu- facturing program also includes TiC-based cermet tool grades and ceramic coated tools.

The Fine Ceramics Division of the parent company makes alumina and nitride ceramic products as well as ceramic substrate for use in semiconductor modules. The alumina ceramics are used both for electrical applications (e.g., as insulators and sealing parts) and for structural applications. Among the nitrides, AlN is used as semiconductor substrate and Si_3N_4 mainly as structural elements.

Both Toshiba Ceramics and Toshiba Tungaloy, like other subsidiaries, are operated as fully independent companies. They have their own technology and R&D resources and market their products through own sales organizations. Coordination with the internal divisions takes place mainly through regular top-level meetings organized by the Planning Office of the Material & Components Group. On these occasions the divisional and subsidiary managers discuss matters of common interest, such as the structure and long-term strategy of the entire group.

R&D organization: general structure

In order to maintain its position at the cutting edge of new technology Toshiba has adopted a policy to spend around 6 percent of its total sales revenues each year on R&D regardless of business fluctuations (*Toshiba Today '90*, 1990, p. 7). The R&D activities are functionally organized into a three-layer structure. The core is the Research & Development Center in Kawasaki, which focuses on basic and advanced research projects expected to result in applications five to ten years ahead. The R&D Center presently consists of twelve different laboratories, one of them being the Metals and Ceramics Laboratory (see Figure 5.3). Attached to the various business groups are eight Development Engineering Laboratories, which conduct more practical and product-oriented development work. One of them is the New Material Engineering Laboratory, which belongs to the Material & Components Group. Finally, each operating division has its own engineering department.

The policy of Toshiba is that 1 percent of group sales (i.e., 15–20 percent of total R&D expenditure) should be allocated directly to the R&D Center. The rest, around 5 percent of sales, should go to the business groups (Hälldahl, 1989, pp. 19–20).

About half of the budget for the R&D Center comes from the corporate headquarters (i.e., the 1 percent mentioned above) and

RESEARCH AND DEVELOPMENT CENTER

- Advanced Research Laboratory
- Metals and Ceramics Laboratory
- Chemical Laboratory
- Materials Application Department
- Electron Devices Laboratory
- Display Devices Laboratory
- Electronics Equipment Laboratory
- Video Systems & Technology Laboratory
- Information Systems Laboratory
- Energy Science and Technology Laboratory
- Mechanical Engineering Laboratory

DEVELOPMENT ENGINEERING LABORATORIES

- Information and Communication Systems Laboratory
- Medical Engineering Laboratory
- Electron Devices Engineering Laboratory
- Semiconductor Products Engineering Laboratory
- Consumer Products Engineering Laboratory
- Nuclear Engineering Laboratory
- Heavy Apparatus Engineering Laboratory
- New Material Engineering Laboratory

ULSI RESEARCH CENTER

MANUFACTURING ENGINEERING LABORATORY

SYSTEMS & SOFTWARE ENGINEERING LABORATORY

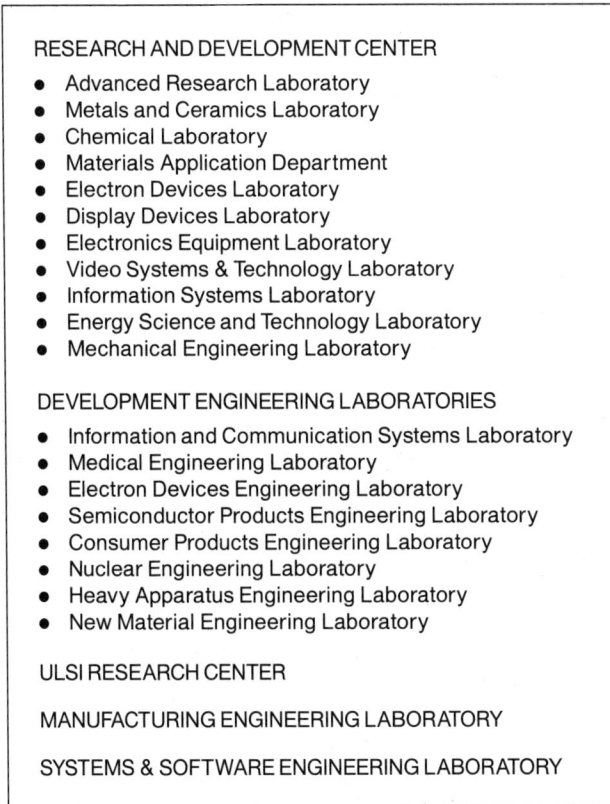

Figure 5.3 Toshiba's R&D laboratories

goes primarily to basic research. The other half comes from the business groups (such as the Material & Components Group) and is paid in proportion to their sales. The direction of these R&D activities is the result of a dialogue between the R&D Center and the business groups and is based on visions held by the different parties involved.

A smaller part of the budget for the R&D Center (approximately 5 percent) is paid by the government as support for national programs that Toshiba has joined. For example, Toshiba is one of sixteen companies participating in the Fine Ceramics Project started by MITI's Agency for Industrial Science and Technology in 1981.

In order to stimulate the creativity in the R&D organization it is considered important that the individual researcher, as being employed in a private company, is given a certain degree of 'academic' freedom. He is therefore allowed to use up to 5 percent of his time to pursue his own personal interests.

R&D organization: fine ceramics

Basic research on fine ceramics is carried out at two laboratories within the corporate R&D Center: the Metals and Ceramics Laboratory, which among other materials is working on structural ceramics, and the Display Devices Laboratory. The latter concentrates on certain types of electronic applications such as semiconductor substrates and IC packages.

Within the New Material Engineering Laboratory there is a Fine Ceramics Department which carries out more applied research than the two above-mentioned laboratories. It is located in the same premises as the production plant, which is part of the Keihin Product Operations (located near Kawasaki).

The engineering department within the Fine Ceramics Division has two main functions. One is to develop new commercial products based on results from the R&D Center and the New Material Engineering Laboratory. The other task is production engineering.

In total there are more than 100 people working on fine ceramics-related R&D within the parent company. Given the multidisciplinary nature of the field the R&D work is normally organized in projects with representatives of the R&D Center, the New Material Engineering Laboratory and the Division. There are presently five big projects and a larger number of small ones. If required, and this is often the case in big projects, representatives of user divisions are also included as members or even leaders in the project organization.

Toshiba Ceramics and Toshiba Tungaloy are both totally independent from a R&D point of view, but have contacts, mainly of an informal nature, with the corporate and business group laboratories. In certain cases formalized research cooperation and technology transfer have taken place between the parent company and the subsidiaries. In case there is a conflict of interest between companies, the issue is brought up before the Group Management, which is responsible for coordinating the activities.

5.4 DEVELOPMENT OF NITRIDE-BASED CERAMICS IN TOSHIBA

Early basic research at the R&D Center

In 1962 Katsutoshi Komeya, a young graduate in chemistry from Yokohama National University, was employed at the R&D Center's Metals and Ceramics Laboratory. There he started to pursue basic research on nitride ceramics, in particular aluminum nitride which had interesting corrosion-resistance properties. A survey of the literature had showed that there were very few scientific publications on aluminum nitride and silicon nitride, and this gave Dr Komeya an opportunity to establish a leading position in this field. The objective of the research, which at this stage was strongly experimental and accompanied by trial and error, was to learn how to make a nitride ceramic material with high density and good mechanical properties. The availability of a fine powder of high quality and the development of an effective sintering technique were important prerequisites in order to reach that goal.

One of the main problems was to find out how to densify the powder into a compact material. At this point in time nobody knew how to do that. It was realized that if nitride ceramics was to be useful in practical applications, which was the long-term goal of the research, the densification problem had to be solved first. After that other characteristics, such as the bending strength and the toughness, had to be improved.

The usage of additives, mixed with the nitride powder prior to granulation and forming (see Figure 5.1), is one of the means used to obtain a high degree of densification in the sintering process. In his search for a suitable additive Dr Komeya made a great number of experiments where he tested various compounds. During this period he had a lot of contacts with other research teams within the R&D Center who supplied him with different additives to test. One of these groups was working on the development of fluorescent materials for color television and was, among other compounds, using so-called rare earth oxides (Y_2O_3, CeO_2, LaO, etc.). The testing of these compounds led to the important discovery that yttria (Y_2O_3) was an effective additive. By sintering silicon nitride powder together with trace amounts of yttria a dense material with a needle-like crystal structure and improved strength and toughness could be obtained (see Figure 5.4). This critical discovery occurred

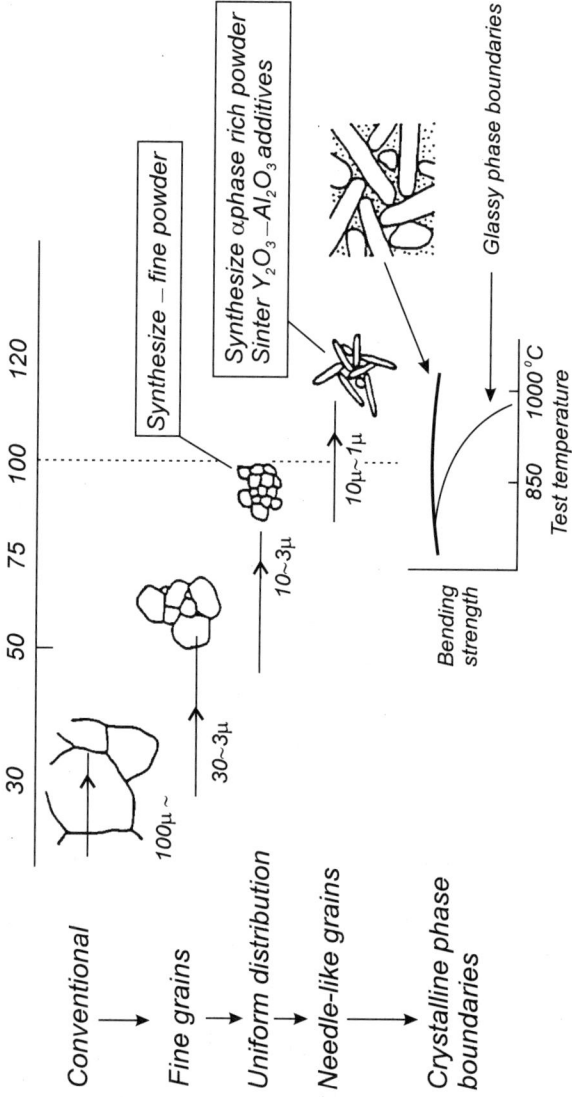

Figure 5.4 High-strength silicon nitride ceramics
Source: Toshiba Corporation

around 1970 and, together with other related discoveries made by Dr Komeya and his co-workers, meant a major step forward in the development of high-performance silicon nitride ceramics.

In commenting on the discovery of yttria, Dr Komeya emphasizes the importance of trial and error in the experimental process. He believes that the trial and error approach is the best way to gain knowledge and make progress in this kind of materials research. He also points out that the finding of yttria was a coincidence, because there was such a tremendous number of conceivable elements and compounds that could be used as additives. But it should also be noted that this coincidence was made possible thanks to the large R&D organization of Toshiba, which facilitated close intra-company interaction with other laboratories and research groups.

A group-wide research project is started

Up till 1970 the activities of Dr Komeya and his colleagues within the R&D Center had been seen as pure basic research. At this time there was no specific policy within Toshiba to develop nitride ceramics. Instead, the research was carried out because Dr Komeya, among others, had a strong commitment to it and was determined, as a scientist, to occupy a position as world leader in the field.[2] It was possible to pursue this kind of exploratory research thanks to the environment of freedom which existed within the R&D Center. As pointed out by one Toshiba manager this kind of environment is very effective in creating inventions and, as a matter of fact, one of the hidden reasons behind Toshiba's successful development of silicon nitride ceramics.

From around 1970 Toshiba's spending on nitride ceramics research increased and the work was broadened to include several other parts of the Toshiba Group (besides the R&D Center). There were several motives for this. First, the successful research of Dr Komeya had contributed to the establishment of a firm knowledge base which could be taken as a starting point for more goal-oriented research and development work. In addition, Dr Komeya had already applied for several basic patents.

Second, it was expected that the development of fine ceramics would have favorable effects on several of Toshiba's key businesses such as heavy electrical apparatus and electronic components. For instance, nitride ceramics was thought to hold the future key to improved efficiency of engines and gas turbines. There was a consensus in the company that if new heat-resistant materials could be developed, then it would also be easy to find applications.

But at the same time it was realized that many technical problems remained to be solved and that several different competencies would be needed. It would thus be extremely difficult for a single company to succeed alone. In the case of Toshiba, the solution was intra-group cooperation. An informal group of companies and laboratories possessing complementary technologies was therefore formed. Core members of this group were the R&D Center, the Metal Products Division (from which the present Fine Ceramics Division later spun off), and Toshiba Ceramics.

The establishment of this informal group in 1970 can be seen as the formal start of a project, in the sense of a more organized and goal-oriented development venture. It should be noted, though, that in Japan the definition of a project is normally not so clear.

As is illustrated in Figure 5.5 the research carried out during the early 1970s was still relatively basic in nature. The focus of the research was to control the crystal structure formation. Important problems had to do with the quality of the powdered raw material and the treatment and mixing of powders prior to sintering. As there was no suitable powder available in the market, the R&D Center, working on the problem, had to search intensively within the Toshiba Group to find potential suppliers of the powder, and test equipment as well. Toshiba Ceramics turned out to have useful technology and succeeded in producing a good powder.

Technology transfer

A few years later, around 1973/4, it was decided that the nitride technology accumulated at the R&D Center would be transferred to the operating units and be further developed into commercial products. The powder technology was given to Toshiba Ceramics and the sintering technology to the Metal Products Division (later Fine Ceramics Division). Behind this division of roles, which was unspoken but implicitly recognized and respected by all parties, lay the realization that powder and components were two different businesses and that duplication of roles would lead to a waste of resources.[3] The task of Toshiba Ceramics, specialized in the manufacturing of fine ceramic materials used in semiconductor devices (mainly SiC products), was thus to make the nitride powder and

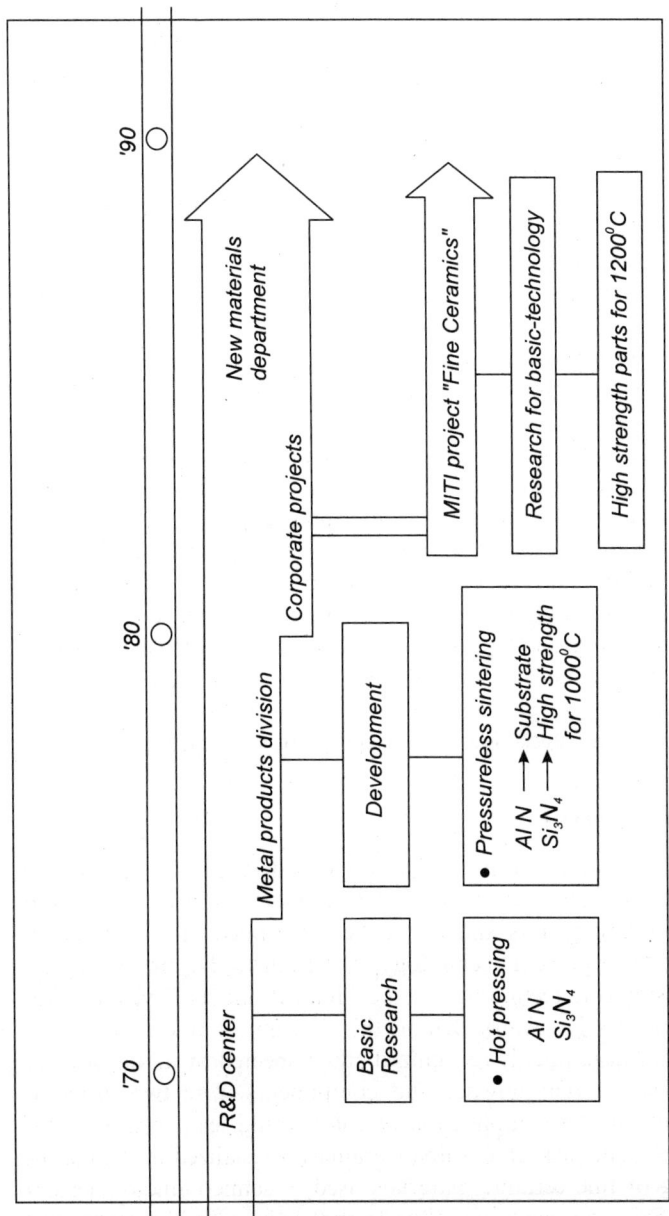

Figure 5.5 Development of nitride ceramics in Toshiba
Source: Toshiba Corporation

sell it to the internal division and to external customers as well. The Metal Products Division was already making structural materials for bearings, gas turbines, motor vehicles, etc., and was therefore better fitted to commercialize the ceramic components. Also Toshiba Tungaloy became actively involved in the commercialization of nitride ceramics, but focused on cutting tool applications.

This type of technology transfer from the R&D Center to the business groups is something which happens quite often in Toshiba. To handle the practical questions and regulate the conditions Toshiba has devised a special system for intra-group technology transfer which includes joint development and technical assistance.

Applied research at the Metal Products Division

At the Metal Products Division Mr Shogo Shimizu, chief engineer, became responsible for developing nitride ceramics. Through the project he became acquainted with Dr Komeya and developed a close and fruitful cooperation with the R&D Center. Especially at the beginning there was a lot of consultation and exchange between the two teams.

An important result of the process development activities carried out at the R&D Center and in the division was that a change could be made from hot pressing to pressureless sintering. Initially, it had been necessary to sinter under high pressure in order to densify the material. But thanks to improvements in the process technology (powder treatment, additives, and control of heating conditions) Toshiba learnt how to achieve a high density under atmospheric pressure. This was a great advantage since it gave a higher productivity and the possibility to make more complex shapes.

There were other manufacturing-related problems which caused difficulties. For example, how the diamond cutting should be carried out without damaging the ceramic parts. This problem was solved by the Manufacturing Engineering Laboratory.

During this stage of development the contacts with other Toshiba companies involved in nitride research were quite loose. The targets were not clearly set and each company was trying to develop technology within its own field of specialization. Thus, the Metal Products Division was not exactly aware of what kind of development was going on in, for example, Toshiba Ceramics,

Toshiba Silicon and Toshiba Tungaloy. On the other hand, the relationships with various user divisions were deepened. For example, there were a lot of discussions with the Energy Division for which silicon nitride was of potential interest as turbine material.

This seeking of contacts was part of a conscious attempt to establish relationships with leading users, within the Toshiba Group as well as outside. Interaction with leading users was seen as an important means to create development opportunities and speed up the commercialization process. As pointed out by Mr Shimizu, it usually takes a long time, often more than ten years, to develop and commercialize a new material.

For the user the introduction of a new material is both risky and costly. Therefore, the Metal Products Division was looking for companies that were prepared to take risks and had financial strength as well. But it turned out to be extremely difficult to talk to the users, as they thought of ceramics as brittle and unreliable materials. Furthermore, they tended to consider ceramics only as a direct replacement for metals not understanding the full benefits offered by the unique properties of ceramics.

The search for commercial applications

The late 1970s and early 1980s was a period characterized by a laborious search for potential users interested in developing nitride ceramics with the Metal Products Division. Contacts already existed with other Toshiba units and in several cases these were translated into joint development activities. In fact, the first commercial application was realized during this period together with the division for heavy electrical apparatus. The part, made of aluminum nitride and characterized by high thermal conductivity and high electric insulation properties, was used as a heat sink substrate for thyristors. The first application of silicon nitride, realized shortly afterwards, was heat-resistant jigs used in the manufacturing of electronic components.

The most extensive internal interaction took place with the Energy Division. They were working on the design and evaluation of turbine components made of various materials. The Metal Products Division contributed by making ceramic pieces and giving information about basic material properties needed by the user. This cooperation has been going on continuously ever since and is regarded by the materials people to have had a big impact on the development of silicon nitride. But in the early 1990s the introduction of ceramic turbine components in commercial production was still expected to lie several years ahead.

Parallel to the internal contacts the Metal Products Division worked hard to establish similar cooperation with external users. They were particularly interested in finding partners in the automotive engine industry, since engine components represented a big potential market for nitride ceramics and Toshiba did not have any such business. There were contacts with many Japanese companies, but it was still difficult to get going. Many of the potential users were interested but thought the time was not ripe and therefore preferred to pursue a wait and see policy. And Toshiba had no power, of course, to force ceramics on the users.

But there were, after all, some companies who were seriously interested in testing ceramics, and in some cases practical trials were indeed carried out as a result of contacts initiated either by Toshiba or the user. Two of these relationships, with Koyo Seiko and Cummins Engine respectively, have developed into more extensive collaborations and led to commercial products.

Koyo Seiko, one of the largest ball-bearing manufacturers in Japan, saw an opportunity in using Toshiba's new ceramic material for wear-resistant parts. The cooperation began in 1983 and resulted, two years later, in Toshiba supplying silicon nitride blanks for balls and races.

By far the most important partner so far has been Cummins Engine. The cooperation between Toshiba and Cummins will be described in more detail later on.

Participation in a MITI project

In order to be able to establish contacts with leading users it was imperative for Toshiba to maintain its position as a technological leader in the industry. This was one important reason why Toshiba joined the national, MITI-sponsored Fine Ceramics Project in 1981.

Toward the end of the 1970s, in the aftermath of the second oil crisis, the Japanese government identified fine ceramics as an important future technology and started to develop policies to promote the fine ceramics industry. In 1981, MITI designated fine ceramics as a priority R&D theme of new materials and took the initiative to start the so-called Fine Ceramics Project. The aim was to develop basic, multi-purpose technology for the utilization of silicon nitride and silicon carbide as structural materials. Thus, the objective was to raise the knowledge level. Development of specific applications was left to the industry.

The R&D work, totally financed by the government, was (and still is) carried out by six national research laboratories and sixteen private companies. The latter were selected out of some applicants by MITI on the basis of interest shown and to what extent they possessed the required technical capabilities in terms of apparatus and people. The group includes powder and parts manufacturers as well as equipment makers and users of ceramic parts. Besides Toshiba, the following companies are participating: Asahi Glass, Denki Kagaku Kogyo, Inoue Japax Research, Ishikawajima-Harima Heavy Industries, Kobe Steel, Kyocera, Krosaki, NGK Insulators, NGK Spark Plug, Nippon Steel, Shinagawa Refractories, Showa Denko, Sumitomo Electric Industries, Toyoda Machine Works, and Toyota Motor Corporation.

The companies have jointly established the Engineering Research Association (ERA) for High Performance Ceramics. It is responsible for planning and coordinating the R&D activities carried out in the private sector. Year by year a plan is made based on previous results and what kind of research activities each company would like to carry out. The plan is ultimately approved, after revision if necessary, by MITI. The ERA is also in charge of promoting information exchange among the participants.

For Toshiba, the participation in this project gave increased possibilities to undertake advanced research on silicon nitride that would enhance its technological capability and attract leading users. The work has been carried out at the R&D Center, the Metal Products Division, and the New Material Engineering Laboratory (which was established in 1987 as a spin off from the Metal Products Division).

These research activities are still going on and it is too early to say what kind of effects they will have on Toshiba's business. So far no results coming out of the MITI project have been applied for commercial purposes, but there is hope this will be possible in the future.

As a by-product, however, Toshiba's participation in the national project, manifesting the priority given to fine ceramics by top management, has made it easier to obtain agreement within the company to commit funds for ceramics research. In parallel to the

Fine Ceramics Project increased resources have thus been invested in other related R&D activities.

Technology licensing

During the 1980s Toshiba signed license agreements with several Japanese ceramics manufacturers who needed Toshiba's patented sintering technology. There were two main reasons behind this transferring of Toshiba's unique knowledge to competitors. One was the economic motive (i.e., the opportunity to make money on licensing).

The other and more important motive was that Toshiba needed help from other manufacturers to develop the market for silicon nitride ceramics. They understood that if Toshiba kept the technology for itself the market growth rate would be low. But if there were several suppliers in the market, belonging to an informal 'technology family' together with Toshiba, then the market would open up more rapidly.

Depending on the economic conditions Toshiba sometimes enters into 'grant back' licensing agreements with other companies. This is often seen as part of a long-term and mutual exchange of technology, which in the long run will be beneficial to both parties. As Toshiba has a policy of not disclosing any information about agreements, no information is available on whether 'grant back' has occurred in the area of fine ceramics.

5.5 CUMMINS ENGINE

Cummins Engine Company, with corporate headquarters in Columbus, Indiana, USA, is one of the world's largest manufacturers of diesel engines. In 1990 the engine business accounted for 69 per cent of its 3.5 billion dollars sales. The company has a complete product line of diesel engines ranging from 76 to 2000 horsepower which are used by a broad variety of on- and off-highway customers. The principal market, however, is the North American heavy-duty truck industry, where every major truck manufacturer offers Cummins engines as standard or optional equipment. The market share was 46 percent in 1990.

The other business areas are Components, Military Systems and Power Systems. The Components Group was formed in 1986 as a result of a diversification program. It designs, manufactures and markets various components and related products to diesel engine manufacturers and end-users around the world. In 1990 over 80 percent of its sales and earnings came from customers other than Cummins.

Since 1989 the Components Group has been engaged in the development, manufacture and marketing of fine ceramic components through a joint venture company, Enceratec Inc., which was formed together with Toshiba. This joint venture operation, which will be described in more detail later on (See pp. 94–5), is the result of a technological cooperation between Toshiba and Cummins which has been going on since the early 1980s. The background of this cooperation will now be described.

Development of a ceramic diesel engine

Around 1974 Cummins began the development of a so-called adiabatic ceramic diesel engine based on a concept invented by Dr Roy Kamo, a second-generation Japanese American. He had been responsible for a gas turbine project at Cummins. In connection to a business trip to Germany he had come to hear about hot-pressed silicon nitride made by Lucas in England and its very promising high-temperature properties. If this material was as good for gas turbines as it was said, it should also be good for the diesel engine, Dr Kamo thought. The basic idea was to use ceramics' excellent insulating and high-temperature strength properties to make a diesel engine without the cooling system (see Figure 5.6). Preliminary calculations showed that it would be possible to achieve fuel savings of up to 30–40 percent in that way. Dr Kamo made a proposal for a development project which, however, was turned down by the management of Cummins. They considered it to be too long-term and risky. But they also said it would be OK if Dr Kamo could get money from the government or other external source.

Dr Kamo contacted a potential user and succeeded in getting a contract for the development of an adiabatic diesel engine for a special type of vehicle. By eliminating the cooling system several advantages could be achieved, such as reduced cost of the engine and the vehicle and improved fuel economy. Within Cummins there was also hope that the project would end up in a standard truck engine, which was the main product of the company. Here the main advantage of the adiabatic engine was the possibility to reduce fuel consumption, since this was a big deal for highway trucks.

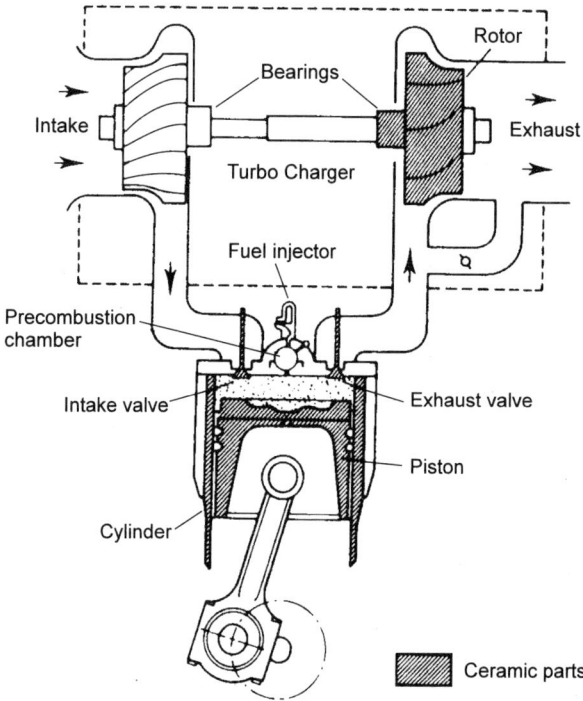

Figure 5.6 Conception of a ceramic diesel engine
Source: Ichinose (1987, p. 58)

From 1974 to 1984 Dr Kamo worked on the development of the adiabatic engine with outside funding. A critical problem was to get a ceramic material which was good enough. Early on Dr Kamo established contacts with all the major fine ceramics manufacturers in America. These showed a lot of interest in the project and supplied various ceramic components, such as cylinder liners, piston heads and turbo charger rotors, which were tested by Dr Kamo and his co-workers. There was a kind of 'ceramic fever' during this period and, although there were those who said it would be impossible to make such big parts in ceramics, there were great expectations among the ceramics manufacturers that the use of the new advanced ceramic materials would revolutionize engine manufacturing. Dr Kamo, however, perceived progress in the US to be too slow, and around 1976 he decided to seek help from abroad, especially from the Japanese fine ceramics industry which he thought to be ahead of its US competitors. During the following years he traveled several times to Japan (as well as to Europe) and visited many companies – Kyocera, NGK Insulators, NTK (NGK Spark Plug), Asahi Glass, Kawasaki Steel, Koransha, and Toshiba among others.

Kyocera, who had a branch in San Diego, were very interested in working with Cummins on the project and also supplied some test pieces. However, the relationship did not develop well since the material was not very good, and at the same time Kyocera went to the Japanese government and asked for money to develop its own adiabatic engine. Instead Cummins came to work with NGK Insulators and Koransha, which were strong in zirconia, and above all with Toshiba. Dr Kamo was very much impressed by Toshiba, which had good research people (Dr Komeya and Dr Tsuge among others). He concluded that Toshiba was the most progressive company and that it had the best material in its hot-pressed silicon nitride. From 1977 on Toshiba supplied several engine components, such as piston caps and exhaust valves, which were tested by Cummins.

By traveling the world and visiting all the major fine ceramics manufacturers Dr Kamo thus managed to build up a vast external contact network which proved to be useful in the adiabatic engine project. But there were at this time no formal alliances between Cummins and any specific suppliers. All deliveries of test material and exchange of information were based on the personal interaction between Dr Kamo and his friends in the supplier firms.

Change of strategy

In spite of intensive support from the ceramics manufacturers and achieved quality improvements, the lack of a sufficiently good ceramic material was still an inhibiting factor in the adiabatic engine project in the early 1980s. It was also realized that Cummins did not have the kind of advanced materials engineering competence necessary to support the project. In 1982 Dr James W. Patten from Battelle Laboratories was therefore hired by Cummins to manage the corporate Materials Engineering Department and to help Dr Kamo.

Dr Patten soon realized that the amount of fuel saving was not going to be as large as previously thought. First, it had become clear to Cummins' engineers that substantial gains in energy efficiency could be made by improving the design of the conventional engine. Second, by doing a more careful thermodynamic analysis it would be possible to reduce the amount of cooling water. In other words, the potential advantages of applying the adiabatic concept to the standard truck engine, which was the main driving force behind Cummins' engagement in the project, would not be as great as had been believed earlier.

This was the first strategic view developed by Dr Patten. A second strategic view was that fine ceramics had more usefulness than just insulation. For example, how could its excellent mechanical properties be used to improve the performance of the conventional engine? After systematic analysis of the potential utility for Cummins and what kinds of material were of interest, three different R&D programs were outlined and subsequently implemented:

1 The use of ceramics for heat insulation.
2 The use of ceramic coating of metals to improve wear resistance.
3 The use of wear-resistant ceramics in structural components.

For each of these programs separate strategies were developed – for example, with regard to what Cummins' involvement with external ceramic manufacturers should be. The analysis of the supplier market had shown that there was no ceramics manufacturer in a leadership position in more than one of these three fields. And furthermore, no company had world leadership for more than one type of material. Different potential partners could thus be identified for different needs.

This new strategy for ceramics, aimed at using the new materials and all the experiences accumulated over the years within the company for the purpose of improving the truck engine, was well on its path from mid-1983. In parallel, the development of a specialty engine continued. However, the emphasis on ceramics in this project was less than before.

In January 1984 Dr Kamo left Cummins to start his own company, Adiabatics Inc. Cummins was interested in taking a 40 percent stake in the company but only on the condition that Adiabatics did not carry out any work for its competitors. Dr Kamo felt that this would tie his hands too much and therefore said no. For some time the relationship between Cummins and Adiabatics was 'not the best', as Dr Kamo put it, but later on both parties recognized that they needed each other. For example,

Adiabatics has developed certain technologies that can be used by Cummins.

The development program for wear-resistant components

The first step in this program, like in the other two, was to make a thorough survey of all potential materials and suppliers. A great amount of information was collected through literature studies and patent search and by talking to people. All potential ceramics suppliers in the world, as well as several government laboratories' were visited. This investigation indicated that silicon nitride was the most promising material, although there were other alternatives, such as zirconia, silicon carbide, alumina, and Sialon.

The patent search had shown that Toshiba had by far the best patent position in silicon nitride. It had some 120 patents, which was almost ten times as much as the nearest competitor. Besides Toshiba there were four other Japanese companies on the list – NGK Insulators, NTK, Asahi Glass, and Kyocera. Among the European producers the most interesting companies were Lucas-Cockson, Feldmühle, and Rosenthal. In the US, Norton had a very strong position. Its silicon nitride, which was considered to be the 'world standard', had already been tested by Cummins and was far and away the best available in the US market. Rumors suggested that Toshiba's material was equally good, but Cummins did not have any hard data. Also on the list were GTE and several other US manufacturers.

The next step was to go and talk to all the potential partners in order to find out whether they were interested and how well they would work with Cummins. Cummins' approach was still rather exploratory at this stage. They had not decided what kind of relationship they wanted with the suppliers but suspected that the best solution would probably be to find an industry leader and form a joint venture with that firm. Dr Kamo played a major role in this phase. He had had contacts with practically all these companies and knew who were the key people and how the companies had performed in the adiabatic engine project.

Cummins received all kinds of responses from the suppliers during these discussions. For example, some were only willing to be pure components suppliers and were not prepared to get directly involved in the development work. Others were interested only if they were allowed to supply all kinds of ceramics. After having sorted out those who lacked technical capability or were not open-minded enough to consider the type of close business relationship Cummins was interested in, five companies remained – three Japanese and two American.

These selected companies were all visited again and a series of meetings were held at senior management level. During the early meetings with Toshiba, one of the remaining candidates, a good fit between the two companies could already be recognized. The senior people turned out to have similar personalities, similar ways of working with people, and common business objectives. For example, both companies were strongly dedicated to go in and develop a ceramic material which had competitive properties and which they could make money on. Neither of them was interested in doing research on ceramics for its own sake. In other words, there was no preconceived notion about what should be done when looking at the facts. If the results showed that one could not make money, which at this point was perceived as a possible conclusion, then the project should be discontinued.

In the fall of 1984 after a long series of discussions and negotiations, which took time partly because of language problems, Cummins decided to choose Toshiba as partner for this program and an agreement was signed in November. 'A decisive factor in our choice of Toshiba undoubtedly was the similarity between the two companies in approaching the business,' Dr Patten pointed out. By that time the other four candidates had been ruled out for various reasons.

As to Kyocera, one of the other potential partners and an extremely successful ceramics manufacturer, Cummins had had a hard time understanding that company. Kyocera was the maverick in the Japanese ceramics industry and in many ways a unique company. 'If we had understood Kyocera better, then the relationship might have come out differently,' Dr Patten said. Later on a fruitful interaction between the two companies was established.

5.6 THE AGREEMENT BETWEEN TOSHIBA AND CUMMINS

The negotiations which preceded the agreement were perceived as very difficult by the Cummins people. 'Several times I thought we were not going to make it,' Dr Patten said. Among important issues which had to be solved were the choice of production location and the ownership of the rights to the research results. For example, it was important for Toshiba to be able to sell the material to other customers, especially the Japanese automakers. And for Cummins it was important to have freedom to work with other suppliers. As explained by Dr Patten much of the mistrust and many of the conflicts which arose during the discussions were caused by pure misunderstanding. 'It happened several times that once we got a clear understanding of what we were talking about the issue disappeared,' he said. These misunderstandings were partly caused by language problems. There were also some 'travel problems' on the part of the Cummins people. This is exemplified by the following episode. After a long meeting in New York the negotiation team of Cummins flew nonstop to Tokyo for a meeting with Toshiba. Dr Patten explained:

> There were many misunderstandings on this occasion, in part because we could not think clearly enough to overcome our communication problems. After several hours' discussion, both sides realized that there was no real fundamental problem. We were very much relieved to reach agreement on the important issues. We had an excellent dinner together afterwards.

As pointed out by one Toshiba manager the language was only part of the problem. Misunderstandings also occurred because of missing information. For example, due to incomplete exchange of information within Toshiba and Cummins every individual involved in the discussions did not have all the facts. He also pointed out that 'language difficulties' do not occur only when the counterpart is a foreign company. 'The language may cause misunderstandings even when we are dealing with other Japanese companies – suppliers or customers. It is because the meaning of words is sometimes different. But usually we can overcome these difficulties and make business,' he said.

After several sessions the cooperative agreement was finally signed in November 1984. It was done at a formal ceremony with attendance of top level managers from both companies. By that time several of the managers had become personal friends.

The agreement was non-exclusive, which made it possible for both Toshiba and Cummins to work with others if they wanted. As to the latter there was a clear intention to focus its efforts with Toshiba, if a fruitful relationship could be put together. The Toshiba people had a similar attitude. For them it was an advantage that they could do business with other customers in parallel. But in practice the agreement meant that Toshiba's efforts to develop silicon nitride applications were mainly to be concentrated on the Cummins project. 'Both were happy with the agreement, and still are,' as one person put it.

The agreement was for three years (i.e., 1985 to 1987). Toshiba had preferred a more long-term contract, which covered a 5–10-year period. However, this was not possible for Cummins, since it had a three-year planning horizon (in principle nothing could be done that took more than three years). But nobody really believed in that. In the discussions both partners had talked about 5–6 years as the necessary time-frame to put ceramic components in commercial production. There was thus a mutual understanding that a new agreement would be made after the initial three years as long as there was enough progress. An advantage with this procedure, as perceived by the Cummins people, was that it would force the parties to make a thorough evaluation of the results before going ahead for a second period. As a matter of fact the original agreement stated that the project should be reconsidered once a year in order to decide whether to continue or stop it.

5.7 TOSHIBA'S AND CUMMINS' JOINT DEVELOPMENT OF WEAR-RESISTANT SILICON NITRIDE COMPONENTS FOR DIESEL ENGINES

After the agreement had been signed in late 1984 a joint project team was put together. It consisted of 3–4 full-time people from Cummins' Materials Engineering Department and 8–9 part-time people from Toshiba's Metal Products Division. In reality, though, more than ten people from Toshiba were actively working on the project.

The work on making and testing silicon nitride components for Cummins' diesel engine had in fact begun even before the agreement. One reason was that both companies wanted to take every opportunity to get to know each other better and enhance the understanding of what problems there were to solve. This work was now intensified.

The procedure was to start by jointly deciding which components to develop. Cummins then purchased these components from Toshiba. The wear resistance of the components was tested both by Cummins and Toshiba, and the results were evaluated by the joint project team. The responsibility for the testing of engines lay basically with Cummins.

As a first step the two companies made a list of components that could be made of silicon nitride and tried to estimate the costs by doing different financial scenarios. The approach was then to focus on the simplest components with high volume. That meant flat and round pieces, such as ball and socket joints, wear pads, valve guides and fuel injection links. The turbocharger wheel and the exhaust valves were not included in the program as they were considered too complex. The rationale behind this strategy to start with the most simple forms, which was quite unique in the industry (most companies did the other way around), was to keep the number of technical problems as few as possible. The most important thing was to achieve reliability in the manufacturing process. The detection of inner cracks in the ceramic parts was difficult and costly, especially if the shape was complex. When the shape was simple it was easier to check the quality, and the inspection cost could be reduced.

One of the most important points in the collaboration had to do with the design of the ceramic parts. At the outset Cummins' components were designed for metal, based on traditional design data. But in order to make use of the superior properties of ceramics at least some minor changes were necessary. Cummins thus had to put efforts into redesigning its components.

This was a dynamic and exploratory phase where Toshiba concentrated mainly on developing the manufacturing process and Cummins on the designing and implementation of the components. Neither Toshiba nor Cummins had any experience of this kind of application and felt that they were breaking new ground. They were quite confident that the wear resistance would be good, but they did not know for sure. And there were a lot of uncertainties about what would happen in the engine. For example, there was no notion at all of the effects of impact between parts (ceramic-on-metal or ceramic-on-ceramic). Another problem had to do with the attachment of ceramic and metallic parts. The cost/benefit ratio was also largely unknown. In summary, there was a set of questions which had to be solved. If there were no solutions there would be no business either.

One problem for the team was that they did not have the possibility to test the ceramic components in actual engines. The Materials Engineering Department of Cummins was a service function which had to work with the Engine Development Groups. Normally it was the latter who performed the testing and evaluation of new components. But they had bad experience of ceramics from the adiabatic engine project and were reluctant to put ceramics in their engines. When it became clear that the Engine Development Groups would not test these new ceramic parts, the Materials Engineering Department decided to acquire its own test cell and engines of the latest design. From late 1986 these engines were filled with ceramic components and were run abusively until they broke. The ceramic components did surprisingly well in general. The results showed, for example, that the impact between parts was not a significant problem. The critical thing was to find a suitable design solution. In about half of the cases it was possible to find satisfactory solutions that would enable the use of ceramics. In the other cases there were engineering problems which could not be solved.

In parallel to the designing, making and testing of various components, Toshiba's Metal Products Division did a great deal of work on the manufacturing process. Among other steps in the process chain (see Figure 5.1), they worked a lot on the forming (e.g., developing the technique of injection molding), the sintering, and the grinding operations. An important problem was to learn how to control the dimension precision and uniformity when making large numbers of components.

Basically independently of the ongoing components development Toshiba's R&D Center continued to pursue basic research on silicon nitride ceramics.[4] This research was more directed toward materials development and did not, at this stage, have any impact on Toshiba's cooperation with Cummins.

Ceramic long links

In 1987 the situation was that the team had favorable performance data for a number of engine components but no customer (end-user). In addition, there was still a lot of uncertainty about the cost and a lack of experience from practical use. At this point in time, however, Cummins had some serious engine component wear problems which made it necessary to expend great efforts on redesigning these components. Among other things there were problems with wearing of the so-called long links in the mechanical fuel injector (see Figure 5.7). These links are small but critical components

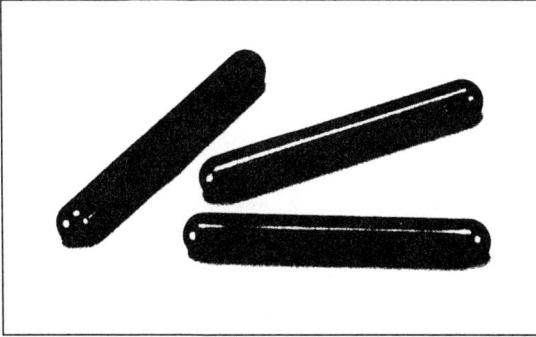

Figure 5.7 Ceramic links for diesel engines
Source: Enceratec

important for the functioning of the engine. Excessive wear of these links leads to power loss and deteriorated fuel efficiency, which of course is negative for the customers (truck owners).

This situation offered an opportunity to try some of the ceramic links based on the data available from previous testing. It was thus decided to make a first field test on 50–60 engines (i.e., some 300 links). The customers were all informed about the test and supported by an emergency system (they could call for assistance at any moment). As a curiosity it can be mentioned that Cummins lost track of which engines had been equipped with ceramic links. But fortunately none of them failed, so nobody knows to this day where they had gone. Two other field tests were subsequently carried out, also with a successful outcome. The customers then began to be aware of the quality of ceramic links and started to demand that their engines be equipped with such links. Some customers even called on the company's president to request these links.

When all this happened the Engine Group could no longer resist ceramics and in 1989, after two years' field testing, they began to use the ceramic links starting with the most critical customers and the highest horsepower engines. The market introduction was done gradually and in a controlled fashion, in reality treated as a field test. It took about one year to reach full production. Since 1991 all Cummins' engines which use mechanical fuel injectors are equipped with ceramic links.

Parallel activities

Parallel to the field testing of the ceramic links Toshiba and Cummins continued to develop other components for the diesel engine. By early 1992, two additional, 'ball type', ceramic components had been introduced in commercial production by Cummins. One is a ceramic ball for a ball-bearing used in an electronic fuel control governor. The other is a check ball used in Cummins' new electronic fuel injector.

Although Toshiba's development efforts have been focused on the cooperation of Cummins, contacts have also been sought with other potential customers, primarily in Japan. The approach is similar to the one employed with Cummins – that is, to search for problems which can be solved by using ceramics. That is seen as one way of escaping the cost issue. Given the results and experience from the Cummins project, diesel engine manufacturers naturally belong to the target group, but other types of applications are also considered.

Since 1990 Toshiba has been trying to develop the US market in a similar fashion. This joint effort with Cummins is described in the following section.

Enceratec

In 1989 Toshiba and Cummins agreed to form Engineering Ceramic Technologies, Inc. (Enceratec), a joint venture company located in Columbus, Indiana. Its main task is to market ceramic components in the US. There were two main reasons behind this decision. First, Toshiba and Cummins felt they had learnt how to manufacture high quality silicon nitride components successfully. They had got good data, a good understanding of the material and the applications, and a good capability to solve engineering problems. There was nobody else in the world who had these competencies. Second, Toshiba had idle capacity in its production plant and wanted to bring in new customers. This was also of interest to Cummins as the cost of the components it bought from Toshiba was related to the capacity utilization.

Enceratec is owned on a 50/50 basis by Cummins' Components Group and Toshiba's Material & Components Group. The staff consists of four people – three engineers (two from Cummins and one from Toshiba) who are specialists in designing and manufacturing ceramic components, and one secretary.

Enceratec is currently involved in two different businesses. One is sales of ceramic ball blanks for ball-bearings. This is a product which had been developed by Toshiba in Japan and is now considered to be fully developed. It is expected to have a bright future. The other business is the designing, engineering and marketing of ceramic wear parts and component systems. So far the long link is the only volume product. The ceramic components are not merely sold to Cummins but to other diesel engine manufacturers as well (the objective of Cummins' Components Group companies is to sell at least 50 percent of their output externally, and there are no constraints on the customer base). Thus Cummins' three main competitors in the North American market, Caterpillar, Detroit Diesel and Mack Trucks, are among the customers. Several other components for engine and other applications are in the development or demonstration stage. Many potential customers from a wide range of industries have showed interest in what Enceratec can offer in terms of products and engineering services. However, manufacturing cost is still a critical factor which slows down the rate of commercialization. The Enceratec people are therefore convinced that if the cost scenario can be improved, then it will also be possible to increase the sales volume substantially.

In the opinion of Cummins, manufacturing operations should be started in the US as soon as there are pre-established customers and products, and the business volume is big enough to support local production. The Cummins people expect that the building of a manufacturing facility in the US would contribute to spur sales in the North American market. As pointed out by one Toshiba manager, it would be an advantage also for Toshiba to establish local production, since the US customers often prefer to have a US source. If the volume would rise fast, then the Japanese factory could be used as a back-up plant.

Some comments on the relationship between Toshiba and Cummins

People in both companies agree that the good cultural fit is one of the main reasons why Toshiba and Cummins succeeded in developing such a fruitful cooperation. It was not only the senior managers who got along well. As testified by Dr Patten, and others, there are cultural similarities at all levels in the organization from top management and down. 'We have a similar way of looking at the world and how we treat the people,' he said and continued:

'There are other companies, Japanese as well as American, we cannot work with due to too large differences in management culture.'

But there are also differences between the two companies. While Cummins is a very decentralized company where each manager is expected to make his/her own decisions, decision-making in Toshiba (like in other big Japanese corporations) takes place at a higher level in the hierarchy. This has made it necessary for the Cummins people to have good contacts with the senior managers in Toshiba, i.e., the head of the Material & Components Group and those below.

The relationship is characterized by a complex pattern of interaction. There are many people involved on both sides. And there are numerous channels of communication and a lot of distributed information exchange. Toshiba, for example, has parallel contacts with the Materials Engineering Department, The Engine Group, plant managers, Enceratec, etc. As a consequence there are a lot of individuals in both companies who have only partial information about the relationship and incomplete knowledge about the functioning of the partner's organization. It is an inevitable effect of such a complexity that misunderstandings and dividing opinions will occur from time to time.

As an example of such an 'issue', which is now eliminated from the agenda, it can be mentioned that there were people at Cummins who perceived information flow from below and upwards in Toshiba to be unsatisfactory. Therefore, in order to have certain problems in the project solved they felt the need to review them with the senior managers. After having explained to the Cummins people how Toshiba's organization works this misunderstanding disappeared. Now there are other 'issues' instead which have to be solved in a similar way; that is, by coming together and explaining and discussing the concepts and philosophies of the two companies.

Another consequence of the large number of people involved, which from time to time has caused some confusion, is that it is difficult to identify 'the opinion of Toshiba' or 'the opinion of Cummins'. In reality there are several different opinions on the project within both companies.

A common practice in large Japanese corporations is the frequent rotation of managers in the organization, and Toshiba is no exception in this respect. For the Cummins people, working in a more stable organization, these personnel changes in Toshiba mean that they often have to build new personal relationships in order to maintain effective channels to the decision-making level.

5.8 THE CURRENT SITUATION

By early 1992 three ceramic components, i.e. the long link and the two ball-type components, had been introduced in commercial production at Cummins. There are several other components with acceptable performance, but they are currently too expensive to be attractive for substitution. They would only be applied if there was a major technical problem which required their use.

What hinders the wider usage of ceramic components by Cummins is thus the cost/benefit analysis which is still not favorable enough. From Cummins' point of view all engineering problems have been solved and the main problem now is to reduce the manufacturing cost.

As in every buyer–seller relationship the price is a matter of opinion. It is normal that the customer, i.e. Cummins in this case, wants to have a lower price, while the supplier wants a higher price. As explained by Mr Masato Sakai, senior manager within the Planning Office of Toshiba's Material & Components Group, the cost/price issue is complex. It is not only a technical problem, but also related to volume and time. For example, the business slow-down in the US has led to decreasing production volume for the long link (which in turn has led to higher manufacturing cost for Toshiba) and in addition put Cummins under strong pressure to reduce costs.

Mr Sakai also points out that the cost/price issue is problematic in almost all new materials development. In general, the cost of the new material is high, because of R&D expenditures, low production volume (i.e., lack of scale economy), and undeveloped manufacturing technology. At the same time the new material has to compete with old and mature materials which are produced in large quantities and at low cost in rational plants. This problem is reflected in the difficulties often encountered by companies trying to expand new material businesses into large-scale operations.

The cost issue is perceived to be a shared problem for Toshiba and Cummins and is currently being discussed in the collaborative spirit of understanding developed over time between the two companies. They are now in the process of devising appropriate strategies to deal with the cost issue through aggressive joint activities.

These will take place within the frame of the formal cooperative agreement, which has been renewed every year since the start in 1984.

As to Cummins, 90–95 percent of its development efforts concerning structural ceramics are done together with Toshiba, which is still considered to be the main partner in this area. Besides the cooperation with Toshiba, Cummins is evaluating some components made by other suppliers. If the other two ceramics programs are taken account of, Toshiba's share would represent about 50 percent. With regard to ceramics coating, for example, Cummins is pursuing similar joint development with a US company.

So far Cummins is the only diesel engine manufacturer which has been successful in developing and introducing wear-resistant ceramic components. Other American manufacturers have tried but not yet reached commercial production. The competitors seem to have used a more experimental approach compared to Cummins. The Cummins people think their own approach, involving more fundamental analysis of design and function, is one of the key factors behind their success.

For Toshiba the close cooperation with Cummins has contributed to strengthen its position as a technological leader in the field of structural fine ceramics. According to independent Japanese specialists in the fine ceramics industry there are six leading suppliers of silicon nitride in the world. They are Kyocera, NGK Insulators, NTK, and Toshiba from Japan, Norton from the United States, and the German ESK (a subsidiary of Hoechst). However, according to these sources the two last-mentioned manufacturers are not as strong as the Japanese producers.

Toshiba's commercialization strategy differs from the strategies of its competitors in its focus on wear parts, such as bearings and diesel engine components. This choice is mainly a result of Toshiba's cooperation with Koyo Seiko and Cummins, but it also fitted the development philosophy of the ceramics people in the company. The other leading manufacturers have to a larger extent chosen to concentrate their efforts on the turbocharger rotor.[5] So far this is the only 'hot' ceramic component which has been commercialized. Toshiba did not consider the turbocharger rotor to be sufficiently attractive from a business point of view. Instead, it is concentrating its development of high-temperature applications on the gas turbine. This is a joint venture with the Energy Division as was mentioned earlier.

In spite of the successful technological development achieved by Toshiba in cooperation with its partners, sales of nitride ceramics are still modest and the real commercial breakthrough probably lies several years ahead. It can be noted, though, that according to MITI's current vision for fine ceramics, the market for structural ceramics is expected to demonstrate a rapid growth in the 1990s and above all in the twenty-first century (Ishiguro, 1991).

Toshiba's view of the development of fine ceramics is that this activity must continue because it is a strategic material for the future. The main driving force is that fine ceramics (like other 'new materials') will have an impact on several of Toshiba's main products (turbines, heavy electrical apparatus, semiconductor devices, etc.). The Material & Components Group thus has a mission from the top management to develop new material technology for internal use: 'That is why we exist,' commented Mr Sakai. But there is also an explicit objective to develop external sales of fine ceramics. The reason is twofold. First, it is one way of increasing the market growth rate. Second, the ceramics business offers opportunities to make money in the future.

Toshiba's development of structural fine ceramics is well in line with the current policy of the Japanese government. In spite of the slow growth of the fine ceramics industry during the 1980s, which has caused some disappointment among certain researchers, business managers and policy-makers, MITI is still optimistic about the future development. At the same time MITI recognizes the enormous technical problems and the need for a long-term perspective. In order to stimulate researchers and industrial companies to continue their efforts MITI has therefore developed policies to promote the fine ceramics industry. Sponsoring of national research projects and other R&D activities is one method. But that is not considered to be enough to create a commercial breakthrough. MITI is convinced that development of practical applications will require more cooperation among companies, especially between ceramics manufacturers and potential users in the automotive and electric power industries. This kind of interaction is stimulated, *inter alia*, by supporting industry cooperation via the Japan Fine Ceramics Association (JFCA). It is a private trade association which at present has more than 200 regular and associate members (including manufacturers as well as users and equipment suppliers). JFCA is working to expand attractive fine ceramics businesses through promotion of exchanges and dissemination of information between companies. It also carries out various surveys of market and R&D trends and other issues related to fine ceramics.

5.9 SOME COMMENTS ON THE TOSHIBA CASE

Like the preceding case this one is an example of fruitful technological cooperation between a supplier and a customer. But the context and prerequisites are quite different. The Nippon Steel case deals with the development of a new steel product intended for an existing application. The development took place within an old and well-established relationship, the stability and closeness of which largely facilitated the interaction and the achievement of a successful outcome. By contrast, the present case deals with a completely new type of material which requires a revolutionary new manufacturing process.[6] Scientific discoveries made in the company's corporate research laboratory constituted the starting point for the development of a commercial product. Although future uses could easily be conceived of (such as the gas turbine), there were no existing ceramic applications or customer relationships that could be built upon. But in order to reach the ultimate goal of developing a commercial product that money could be made on, it was necessary for Toshiba to link their own development activities to other activities outside the company – in particular on the user side. The systematic searching for suitable partners and the establishment of cooperative relationships therefore became important elements of the innovation process.

A striking outcome of this search process was the establishment of a partnership with an American firm. Normally, one would expect a Japanese company to cooperate with domestic customers in a case like this. What we have here is thus an example of R&D cooperation within an international buyer–seller relationship. The relationship and the outcome of the joint development work had strategic importance for both companies.

There are several other interaction- and network-related aspects of technological innovation that are illustrated by this case. One is the gradual building up of a cooperative relationship through successively increasing commitments and joint activities. Another one is the importance of technology sharing. Furthermore, the case illustrates the need for a long-term approach and perseverance in developing and introducing new advanced materials like structural fine ceramics. Obviously, this type of undertaking can only be made by large and forward-looking companies that can afford to invest considerable resources over many years without looking too closely at the short-term return.

Relationship effects

In Chapter 2 three different relationship effects were described: knowledge creation, activity coordination, and resource mobilization. Toshiba has used its relationship with Cummins for all three purposes (and vice versa). It was by combining Toshiba's knowledge of materials and ceramics manufacturing with Cummins' knowledge about the manufacturing and usage of engine components that it was possible to learn how to make high quality silicon nitride components that could be used in practical applications. It is unlikely that either of the two companies could have achieved this goal on its own.

It was by letting people from the two companies work on the task within a joint project that the two companies' resources (human as well as equipment) could be brought together, adapted and further developed. That was the most important function of the relationship. But in order to make the development process efficient it was also important to use the relationship for activity coordination. There were many different activities, such as designing, manufacturing, testing, etc., that had to be coordinated. In addition, these activities were controlled by several relatively independent organizational units within Toshiba and Cummins, and this made the coordination process more difficult.

Third, a lot of mobilization effort had to be carried out in order to move the project forward. Mobilization activities took place not only in the relationship but also internally within the two companies.

Chapter 6

Case analysis

In this chapter we shall return to the management issues identified in the concluding section of Chapter 2. The questions raised in that section will be discussed against the background of the two cases. To begin with, the focus will be on the companies' general approach to external technological cooperation with other actors in the network. That discussion will then be followed by a section dealing with the problem of selecting partner(s). Third, the problem of handling individual relationships will be discussed.

6.1 DEGREE OF COOPERATION AND INTEGRATION WITH THE NETWORK

Although a company (or business unit) has a certain freedom when it comes to choosing a cooperative approach to technological development within a certain field of its operations, this choice is largely influenced by the characteristics of the industry or network, the position of the company in that network, and its overall technology strategy in the field. It is easily recognized, as has already been pointed out, that the situations of Nippon Steel and Toshiba, respectively, are quite different. Let us start by discussing the case of Nippon Steel and the development of coated steel sheet products.

The Nippon Steel case

This network, whose main actors are the steelmakers and the users of corrosion resistant steel sheet, is a very stable one. There is a relatively constant set of producers and users who are related to one another through business relationships that are in many cases close, long lasting and stable. This state of affairs can be explained, of course, by the relative maturity of the technology (both on the supplier and on the user side) as well as the large scale-advantages and the high capital intensity. The network started to develop several decades ago and the actors have had plenty of time to build up close relationships involving a lot of activity links, resource ties and actor bonds. This process has taken place especially in major industrialized countries (i.e., more or less nationally delimited networks have been formed in countries like Japan, Germany, Great Britain, France and the US).

Japan can thus be said to have its own national network for coated steel sheet. The key actors are the five leading steel producers (i.e., besides Nippon Steel, NKK, Kawasaki Steel, Kobe Steel and Sumitomo Metals), and large user firms, primarily the automakers, the manufacturers of household appliances and the big construction companies. Also, on the user side the number of important actors is limited, though it is higher than the number on the supplier side.

This network, like the corresponding ones in Europe for example, is characterized by a certain degree of heterogeneity in terms of the differing demands various users make on the properties of the steel products. There are not only differences between the sectors, but also between companies within a sector. Thus, the automakers differ in their requirements and wishes resulting from differences in production equipment, automobile design and corrosion protection philosophy (this in spite of the fact that from the consumers' point of view the automobiles are quite similar in terms of their functions, features, quality and appearance).

Given the heterogeneity of the market and the power of major buyers (in terms of their purchasing volumes) a steel supplier like Nippon Steel, who aspires to be a market leader, is more or less forced to adopt a technology strategy that implies development cooperation with customers. However, due to the scale advantages in steelmaking, a far-reaching product adaptation for every customer would be too costly. Therefore, it is natural and logical for Nippon Steel to choose a strategy where it pursues product development cooperation with its 10–20 major customers, while the others have to put up with existing products (developed together with key customers).

Nippon Steel's relationships with the large customers are characterized by strong activity links and resource ties between the production systems. The existence of permanent joint R&D organizations with several of these customers also gives evidence of strong actor bonds. The cooperative relationships are to a substantial extent the result of previous technological exchange. At the same time, though, the existence of these strong links, ties and bonds gives opportunities for technological exchange that are natural to exploit. As we have seen, it is also a conscious policy of Nippon Steel to pursue its product development in close cooperation with major customers (not least in the field of coated steel sheet). The case describes an example of technological exchange within one relationship, i.e. with Toyota. Toyota is Nippon Steel's largest customer, which undoubtedly makes this relationship a particularly important one, but it is not unique with regard to its substance and function.

Obviously, Nippon Steel uses these relationships to obtain all of the three effects discussed in Chapter 2. The existence of the permanent joint R&D groups leads to activity coordination and resource mobilization when needed. The temporary teams which are established on a project basis help to bring the two companies' human and other resources together. By letting engineers from the two companies, representing different competencies, work together on a common task interactive knowledge effects can be generated. In the case of DUREXCELITE Toyota contributed, among other things, valuable knowledge and facilities for testing and using coated steel sheet. This enabled the two companies to develop a new innovative product that was well adapted to the current customer requirements.

It is true that the original invention that triggered the DUREXCELITE project was not a direct effect of interaction between Nippon Steel and Toyota. But it is also true that the invention was made possible thanks to the inventor's long experience of working closely with customers, particularly with Toyota. In theoretical terms, we can describe this as a resource tie (which was explicitly used by the company to create new technology).

The above-mentioned kinds of application knowledge and testing facilities are often immensely valuable when developing new industrial products.[1] For Nippon Steel, being a steel producer, it is difficult and costly to acquire and maintain these resources, but through close cooperative relationships with leading customers it can get access to them. The experience of the first corporation-wide R&D organizations established with a couple of key customers in the late 1970s proved to be very positive, and since then the company has therefore continued to build up similar cooperation forms with other important customers.

As has already been concluded, cooperation with customers in product development is not unusual. In the area of specialty steel, particularly, this is a common element of the R&D strategy. But what can be learnt from the Nippon Steel case is the advantage of institutionalizing the technological cooperation on a company-wide level. It is probable that many other companies would have much to gain from adopting such a systematic and conscious approach to customer cooperation. This recommendation to overhaul the R&D strategy pertains to steelmakers, of course, but also to other industrial goods manufacturers who are operating in networks with similar characteristics.

The Toshiba case

The development situation prevailing in this case is quite different from that in Nippon Steel. Although Toshiba is an old company and an old manufacturer of structural materials, the case deals with the inception and growth of a new business activity – the manufacturing and sales of advanced ceramics for structural usage. Structural fine ceramics is a relatively new class of materials and the industrial network is not at all as well developed and stable as in the case of coated steel sheet.[2] As a matter of fact the industrial network began to develop in the early 1970s, during the same period in which Toshiba made its first attempts to commercialize its own technology.

Like the previous development story this one was triggered by an internal invention. But unlike the Nippon Steel case Toshiba's early breakthrough invention did not come up as a direct response to customer needs expressed in an existing business relationship. Instead, it was the result of basic research carried out in the company's corporate research laboratory. The technology built up through this research was perceived by Toshiba to offer interesting business opportunities.

For the same reasons that Nippon Steel realized the need to cooperate with a customer in developing and testing DUREXCELITE, it was recognized within Toshiba's Metal Products Division (later on the Fine Ceramics Division) that collaboration with potential users of fine ceramics would be necessary. But at the outset there were no existing customer relationships that could be used, with the exception of some internal customers within the Toshiba Group. However, the case deals primarily with automotive applications for which there were no in-house customers.

While in the DUREXCELITE case the cooperation strategy of the innovating firm was in reality given by the circumstances, the question of how to approach the network was, at least in theory, open in the Toshiba case. The company could choose between trying to develop end-products by itself or establish some kind of R&D cooperation with one or several users. As described, the company chose the latter approach. It was because the managers and engineers within the division realized the necessity of coupling their own product development to the development of concrete customer applications. Due to the unique properties of silicon nitride there was a need to adapt the customers' way of using the material (compared with how they used existing materials, i.e. metallic parts). In other words, the application itself had to be developed. Furthermore, Toshiba needed partners in order to be able to test ceramic automotive parts on a larger scale. Expressed in theoretical terms, there was thus a need for Toshiba to establish activity links and resource ties. These were intended to give several effects, such as knowledge creation and activity coordination. Resource mobilization was also necessary due to the development investments that had to be made by the users.

The network, which in this case seems to be characterized by a relatively high degree of international integration (with tight national densifications of course), thus began to evolve in the 1970s. In the early days the network was, as could be expected, quite loose and unstructured. In Japan as well as in Europe and North America, there were a great number of actors who jumped into the field of fine ceramics in the role of manufacturer, user or researcher/developer. It seems that most of the early relationships among the actors were relatively loose; that is, the resource ties and activity links were not so strong (but there were certainly some exceptions). Cummins, for example, was testing ceramic parts from a large number of American and foreign ceramic suppliers but had no specific partner.

Toshiba's explicit strategy (probably like the strategies of most of its competitors) was to develop commercial products and applications together with users. Although it proved to be rather difficult to get potential users (in the automotive field) to try ceramics,

Toshiba did create interest among some companies and also established a number of weak links (for example with users like Cummins who ordered small quantities of test material and gave more or less thorough feed-back on the performance). However, these limited exchanges were not enough to permit the development of commercial products. What Toshiba needed was a much deeper relationship that contained stronger activity links and resource ties. A prerequisite for establishing this kind of relationship was that the partner should be prepared to invest a considerable amount of resources. As late as the first half of the 1980s, it was still difficult for Toshiba to get these resources mobilized. Despite their interest most potential users played a wait-and-see game, since they thought the right time for investing in fine ceramics had not yet arrived.

The seeking of resource mobilization was thus an important networking activity for Toshiba during a long period. A lot of contacts were established but these did not, for a long time, lead to the kind of relationship that would produce the effects necessary for a successful commercialization. Obviously, Toshiba's membership in the Mitsui group (one of the six major so-called intermarket *keiretsu* in Japan) did not help.[3] This is an interesting observation given the importance to technological innovation attributed to this type of Japanese business groupings by other researchers (see, e.g., Nakatani, 1990; Gerlach, 1992b; Harryson, 1995). The *keiretsu* issue will be further discussed in the final chapter.

It can be concluded that in reality, Toshiba, like Nippon Steel, did not have much of a choice in selecting a cooperative approach toward the network. Because of its dependency on external resources (which would be impossible to build up internally) and the need for activity linking it was imperative to find users to cooperate with. But since there were no established relationships that were close enough, a lot of efforts had to be devoted to the searching for suitable partners and mobilization of resources with these partners. An important result of this process was the establishment of cooperation with Cummins, which we shall come back to in the following section.

Given the need for a relatively extensive technological exchange with the customers, in order to develop large-scale applications, it was obvious that the number of partners had to be limited. This illustrates the importance of the partner selection issue, since different relationships can be expected to yield different effects (cf. the heterogeneity of industrial networks).

Toshiba's cooperative approach in the field of fine ceramics discussed so far only pertains to the development of commercial products (starting from a research-based technology). In parallel to the commercialization efforts, Toshiba has continued its basic and more long-term research at the corporate R&D Center. Here there is not the same need to cooperate with customers since the objective is different; that is, to generate new fundamental knowledge about the material and the manufacturing processes. However, part of this research has been carried out within the frame of a national MITI-sponsored program (and other similar programs financed by the government). Participation in this program has given Toshiba the opportunity to take an active part in collective knowledge creation. There seem to be some activity links among the participants (sixteen companies and national laboratories) but few real resource ties. This explains why relatively few interactive knowledge effects have been produced so far (but that was not the intention of the program). However, the knowledge gained through access to its own and others' research results is highly appreciated by Toshiba. As the scientists working on the MITI project are also involved in other, internal research activities, it is reasonable to assume that the knowledge has been useful, despite the fact that so far no patents from the program have been exploited by Toshiba.[4]

The MITI program has interesting resource mobilization effects. First, there are some internal effects. Thanks to Toshiba's participation in the program (supported by the top management) it has become easier to raise internal funds for ceramics R&D. Second, the government's targeting of structural fine ceramics as a key technology for the future has spurred investments in ceramics technology in the Japanese industry. This is expected to have positive effects on Toshiba's continued efforts to develop cooperative relationships with domestic customers.

Concluding remarks

The discussion has shown that it was natural for both Nippon Steel and Toshiba to seek close product development cooperation with a limited number of customers (just one, given in advance, in the case of Nippon Steel). Against the background of earlier studies, it can be argued that both of these situations, and their consequences for the innovating companies' choice of cooperative strategy, are common in industrial markets in general and in the field of high-performance materials in particular. A lot of companies have learnt, sometimes the hard way through failures, that this is the most effective approach to the development and commercialization of new products. However, the right choice of cooperative strategy is no guarantee of success. The strategy, implicit or explicit, also has to be implemented in a fruitful way, and it is here the issues of partner selection and relationships handling come in.

Before proceeding, it should be added that there are certainly many situations, also in industrial markets, where the described approaches are not appropriate – for example, when developing products that for scale reasons need to be highly standardized and that can be used by customers without adaptation. Certain types of semiconductor components (e.g., memory chips) probably belong to this category. Here, parallel cooperation with other manufacturers, with which the extremely high R&D costs can be shared, seems to be more important than customer cooperation. But nevertheless, good contacts with leading users is also important for these firms in order for them to gain the knowledge of how to formulate R&D goals.

6.2 SELECTION OF PARTNER

In this section, the issue of 'with whom' the company should cooperate will be discussed. The issue has more or less relevance depending on the situation at hand. Thus, in the case of DUREX-CELITE there was in fact no explicit decision made in this respect. The project proposal had come up as a response to the needs of Toyota and there was no reason to consider other partners.

On the corporate level, though, there is of course a kind of choice situation for Nippon Steel. Given its desire to conduct the development of new coated steel products together with customers, the questions are with how many customers should the technological cooperation be carried out and with which specific customers should collaborative relationships be established. But here again, the answers are pretty much given by the circumstances. As already pointed out, there are a few dominant buyers in the domestic market who are technologically strong and active themselves in the development of coated steel sheet products and applications. It is natural to work with them, at least to the extent that these customers are themselves interested in cooperating with Nippon Steel.

A pattern where a company (like Nippon Steel) carries out parallel product development projects with several customers, leading to different products (different coatings in the present case), consumes larger resources for development and production compared with an alternative pattern where a product is developed with one 'lead customer' and then sold to the others (a not unusual strategy among industrial goods manufacturers). However, as already explained such an approach would not be possible for Nippon Steel in the area of coated steel sheet for automotive use. Due to the differentiated product demands in this market the coatings have to be adapted to individual customer needs. Besides the purely technical aspects, the strong competition among certain of these automobile makers, especially between the two 'arch rivals' Nissan and Toyota, would make it impossible to supply them with identical products.

In relation to the smaller customers, there are possibilities to use technology and products that have been developed together with the main customers. However, as illustrated by the DUREXCE-LITE case, this 'connecting' of relationships is not always unproblematic. We shall come back to this later on when discussing the issue of managing relationships.

In the Toshiba case the selection of partners for developing ceramic automotive components was of course an open question. Although the Metal Products Division had working customer relationships for its existing (metallic) products, these were not very useful for the ceramic development, since the applications were different. Toshiba therefore had to build up new relationships from scratch. They knew that they had to find 'leading users' with whom they could establish technological cooperation for product and application development. They also realized that the process of developing commercial products would be a difficult one. Therefore, the kind of partners they were looking for should 'be prepared to take risks and have financial strength'.

The search for partners

As thoroughly described in the Toshiba case, this search process proved to be both lengthy and difficult. The real problem was not so much to select a partner but rather to find someone who was prepared to join Toshiba and invest the necessary resources. Generally speaking, the mutual character of buyer–seller relationships implies that the partner selection is seldom a unidirectional activity. If there is going to be any mutually rewarding exchange both parties have to be serious and make commitments. Therefore, establishing a partnership is as much a question of being selected as to select. This is nicely illustrated by the case.

The first attempts to initiate cooperation with external users were made in the mid-1970s, but failed. The search was intensified from the late 1970s. Despite continued difficulties in getting users to invest, however, these activities resulted in the establishment of some loose relationships. Two of these, with Koyo Seiko and Cummins respectively, would later be turned into collaborative relationships.

The first exchange between Toshiba and Cummins took place in 1977 (the adiabatic project). But it was not until 1984, after Cummins' decision to change its strategy for using ceramics, that the real cooperation began. Here we have an example of a very systematic and conscious selection procedure. Cummins already had contacts and technological exchange with a large number of ceramics manufacturers. But in order to develop wear components and bring them into commercial use Cummins realized the need for closer cooperation with one supplier. They understood the necessity of concentrating the efforts and establishing activity links and resource ties between materials and parts manufacturing on the one hand and parts usage on the other. Due to the limited resources it would be too costly to pursue such cooperation with several suppliers.

Cummins' choice of Toshiba as the most wanted partner thus came out of a systematic selection process where a number of conceivable suppliers were evaluated in a step-wise manner according to several explicit criteria. These criteria did not only take into consideration the potential partners' scientific and technological capabilities but also the prerequisites for developing a relationship having the desired characteristics. Previous experience of dealing with these companies constituted an important source of information.

What we have here is a clear choice situation, which made it possible for Cummins to use a systematic and rational approach. It should be noted, though, that partner choices in industrial markets are not always the result of explicit and 'rational' decision-making processes. On the contrary, previous research has shown that buyer–seller relationships often develop gradually over time. By doing business with each other, companies learn to know each other and make various adaptations, which result, sometimes unconsciously, in the creation of activity links, resource ties and actor bonds. These in turn give favorable conditions for deepening the technological exchange if and when the need arises. In other words, it is not unusual for 'ordinary' business relationships to evolve into collaborative relationships in this way, step by step. It is a process which can take quite a long time. The current relationship between Nippon Steel and Toyota can be seen as the result of such a process which has been going on for decades. The Toshiba case shows, on the other hand, that the process of establishing a partnership under certain conditions can be quite rapid (if we disregard the prehistory between 1977 and 1984).

The selection of a foreign partner

It is remarkable, and a unique feature of this case, that Toshiba's principal partner turned out to be an American firm. Commonly, companies tend to cooperate more often with their domestic customers than with foreign ones. The reasons are obvious. It is interesting to note, however, that this pattern holds even for many of the highly internationalized Swedish companies which export more than 90 percent of their domestic production.[5] That Japanese companies, in general, have most of their R&D partners in Japan is a well-known fact.

In the search for a partner Toshiba first looked at Japanese users and would probably have preferred a domestic partner if there had been one. However, as we know, it was difficult to find Japanese users who were sufficiently interested. Apart from Koyo Seiko, it was not until Cummins proposed a joint development of wear parts for the diesel engine that Toshiba was given the opportunity to develop a deeper cooperative relationship in the field of automotive engines. Cummins had suitable applications and was dedicated to developing and commercializing silicon nitride ceramics. This was the kind of opportunity Toshiba had been looking for, and it was natural to respond to this invitation in a positive way – in spite of the fact that Cummins was not a Japanese company.

Before this happened Toshiba had discussed cooperation with several Japanese companies, but for various reasons these project ideas did not materialize. It can be noted that the Japanese automobile industry showed a keen interest in fine ceramics and in several cases launched their own R&D projects. According to one of the persons interviewed, Toyota Motor Corporation (which like Toshiba is a member of the Mitsui group) at one point in time was in the situation where it had to decide whether to enter into a partnership with an external parts-maker or develop the material in-house. They decided to do the latter. We can only speculate on the outcome, but if Toshiba had succeeded in developing a closer collaboration with Toyota, or one of the other larger Japanese automotive companies, it is possible that Toshiba would have got a different main partner for its development of ceramic engine components. If this had happened it is possible that the development would have gone in a somewhat different direction; we cannot know which one of course. Each company has its own technical issues. Another, hypothetical, partner may not have had wear problems like Cummins. It may, for example, have had heat insulation problems or horsepower problems instead. And this would have required another type of solution.

It is also possible that such a relationship would have evolved differently. For example, Toyota's policy is to control the manufacturing of core components. Probably, unlike Cummins, it would not have relied on Toshiba as sole supplier of ceramic parts but rather would have developed its own parallel manufacturing capability. This kind of sourcing policy, adding an element of competition to the relationship and enhancing the power of the buyer, makes it difficult to be an external supplier to Toyota. It is thus reasonable to assume that a hypothetical relationship between Toshiba and Toyota would have looked quite different to Toshiba's relationship with Cummins. Whether such a relationship would have been better or not for Toshiba is impossible to say.

What would have happened then if Cummins had not existed or for some reason had chosen another partner? The most probable scenario is that Toshiba would have continued its efforts to find a partner within the automotive industry and that it sooner or later would have found someone else to cooperate with. It could have been a Japanese company or a foreign one.

Some conclusions regarding partner selection

The choice of partner, irrespective of how it is made, is obviously a critical moment, or rather a critical stage, in the innovation process. It is critical because of the high degree of heterogeneity that characterizes many industrial networks – i.e., the actors are not identical but differ from each other in various dimensions. Due to this heterogeneity, the outcome of a R&D venture will vary depending on which external activities and resources the company's own activities and resources are combined with. For example, as product and application development often go hand in hand, the selection of customer to cooperate with, and the target application that follows from that choice, can have important consequences for the outcome, such as the product's design, properties or performance and its usefulness in different fields of application. However, because of the uncertainty inherent in all innovative activities and the actors' limited knowledge of the network, these consequences are difficult to foresee. In other words, in many cases it is impossible to know in advance who is 'the best' partner (from technological and other points of view). It is only through trial (and error) that it is possible to find out whether a certain constellation of cooperating actors (two or more) will yield fruitful results.

This does not mean, of course, that companies should not try to act in a rational way. Cummins' choice of Toshiba as partner for the development of silicon nitride is an example of a very systematic and rational selection process. Toshiba's behavior is also quite rational and systematic in its own way; that is, seeking contact with a lot of potential users and then reacting in a powerful way once a suitable opportunity presented itself. Nippon Steel's strategy to develop long-term collaborative relationships with a number of leading customers also seems to be effective, even if in reality it means that the partner choice is often determined in advance.

It is inevitable that randomness often plays an important role in the choice of partner and thereby of development direction. The number of potential combination possibilities in networks is almost unlimited and there are only a few of them that are discovered and given the chance to be explored. Once a choice is made and an interaction process started, the possibility to exploit other combination possibilities is reduced. It is partly because of the always present resource scarcity, partly because the cooperation with a chosen partner may lead to changes in the company's own resources that render them less valuable in other combinations. It may be too drastic to characterize the partner choice as an 'irreversible process', but it is certain that the change of partner in a major R&D undertaking may prove to be extremely difficult and costly (in terms of time and money). But at the same time, the company cannot wait until the best opportunity comes up. It is because the company cannot know, when a certain opportunity is identified, if it really is 'the best one'. It has to act and react knowing that by exploiting a certain opportunity it may be forced to give up other better opportunities that will possibly turn up later on (or these opportunities may in reality never occur because the company has already made its choice).

This importance of randomness in discovering new development opportunities also has other kinds of implications for companies committed to innovation-driven growth. In order to discover new combination possibilities the company should be organized and managed so that an effective information exchange can take place between the customers or suppliers and the company's own technology core. It means that the externally oriented functions – such as purchasing, marketing and after sales service – have to be well integrated with the internal R&D activities. The purchasers and salesmen may for example be used as transmitters of information. But this may not be enough. It may be a great advantage to have the R&D engineers themselves directly involved in customer and supplier contacts. In fact, many companies do that, sometimes in a very systematic way, but probably there are many other companies where the opportunity to use relationships in this way is not optimal.

It has been described how both Toshiba and Cummins were searching for partners. Before making the agreement to join forces both had had contacts with many other companies. But why did these contacts fail to produce partnerships and what was it that made Toshiba and Cummins form such a fruitful combination (but, as explained above, not necessarily 'the best' for either of them)? Let us conclude this section by elaborating a little bit on this question.

It seems that a well-functioning cooperative relationship cannot develop unless there is some kind of 'fit' between the two companies. And this fit must be perceived to be a good one by both companies. As already pointed out, partner choice is never a one-sided action – there must always be two parties involved in the decision. We can distinguish at least four types of fit that are relevant for the kind of technological cooperation we are dealing with in this study. They are. (a) functional fit; (b) strategic fit; (c) organizational fit; and (d) time fit.

Functional fit

Functional fit has to do with the extent to which two companies have complementary resources and activities. For example, Toshiba was looking for autoengine manufacturers who were interested in developing simple-shaped silicon nitride components (thus excluding the turbocharger that most of its competitors were focusing on). Furthermore, the partner should have financial resources that enabled a long-term and risky project. Cummins matched that description quite well. As to Cummins, they were looking for a materials supplier which could help them develop fine ceramics-based wear components for the diesel engine. They had found silicon nitride to be the most promising material for this application, and furthermore that Toshiba had a leading position with regard to that material and was firmly determined to develop commercial applications in cooperation with customers.

The step-wise learning and adaptation process that takes place over time in many buyer–seller relationships may contribute to improve the functional fit between two companies, and in that way increase the prerequisites for establishing a fruitful technological cooperation (at the same time as other conceivable partnerships may become relatively less attractive). Toshiba and Cummins have gradually widened their cooperation, which can be seen as a result of such a process. The good functional fit that seems to exist between Nippon Steel and Toyota is a result of a long-lasting relationship between these two companies.

Strategic fit

The term 'strategic fit' refers to the fit that may or may not exist between two companies' strategies and long-term ambitions – for example with regard to their future positions in the network. Toshiba and Cummins had a common interest in their intention to develop and commercialize silicon nitride ceramics, but they were not competitors. And they were both determined to achieve this goal by establishing close technological cooperation with business partners (i.e., customers and suppliers respectively). It can be noted that some of the other ceramics manufacturers wanted to have another type of relationship with Cummins, which can be interpreted as a less favorable fit. It can also be mentioned that one of the reasons why Cummins' early discussions with Kyocera did not develop into cooperation was Kyocera's plans to develop its own competing adiabatic diesel engine.

Similarly to what may happen to the functional fit, the strategic fit between two companies may be improved as a result of the interaction. Cummins' strategy to make and sell ceramics components to external diesel engine manufacturers through Enceratec, its joint venture with Toshiba, was probably influenced by its cooperation with Toshiba. The two companies are now so closely interwound with each other that it would be very difficult for both of them to change partners.

Organizational fit

The prerequisites for starting a cooperation is also affected by the existence or lack of an organizational fit. It has to do with such factors as organization structure, company culture, management system and so forth. Generally speaking, cooperation is facilitated if there are similarities in these respects.

Although it seems difficult to pinpoint in concrete terms in what ways Toshiba's and Cummins' cultures are similar, representatives of both companies emphasize the importance of this similarity. The good cultural fit which is said to exist did not prevent communication problems from arising during different phases of the cooperation, but they probably helped to solve these problems in a positive way. It is interesting to note that both companies state that there are domestic companies with which they find it more difficult to interact, due to differences in company culture.

Kyocera was one of the alternative partners that Cummins considered. It seems that there was a good functional fit. Another advantage, of organizational character, was that Kyocera had a branch in the US. However, due to the special culture of this company (sometimes described as esoteric), Cummins did not understand Kyocera and chose to eliminate it from the list of candidates. But if the cultural fit had been better it is quite possible that the discussions would have come out differently and resulted in Cummins going for Kyocera instead of Toshiba. This is only speculation, of course.

Time fit

The fourth type of fit that is also necessary, if there is going to be any real cooperation, is the time fit. What it means is that the timing has to be correct, in the sense that both parties have, or are prepared to start, combined development activities at the same time. In both of the investigated cases such a time fit obviously existed. But, for example, if one of the parties has its resources tied up by another activity, has recently invested in another technology, or is already working together with a third party, then there might not be any prerequisites for starting a cooperation even if the functional, strategic and organizational fits are good. This situation may of course change over time. As an example, it can be recalled that many of the Japanese materials users were interested in ceramics but thought the timing to invest was not right due to the immaturity of fine ceramics. Now, when the ceramics technology has improved and there are commercial applications in the market, some of them may change their attitude and be prepared to establish a relationship with Toshiba (but that will probably result in a different type of relationship than Toshiba was looking for back in the 1970s and 1980s).

6.3 MANAGEMENT OF COOPERATIVE RELATIONSHIPS

A typical feature of cooperative relationships that has been stressed in the preceding sections is that they tend to develop gradually over time. The uncertainty of the innovation process makes trust an important condition for close technological cooperation, and trust can only be built over time. For example, the actors often perceive the need to learn to know each other and to 'test' each other in limited exchange episodes before more demanding and risky projects can be undertaken. But it should be well understood that this successive building up of cooperative relationships does not mean that they develop spontaneously and without efforts. The truth is that a relationship does not become effective and profitable unless it is systematically and continuously managed.

There are many different kinds of problems that have to be handled. Some of them have to do with the interaction process itself; for example, how to organize, control and perform the exchange activities. Others have to do with the coordination of the relationship with the company's internal activities and resources. It is important, among other things, that the relationship is technologically, administratively and socially integrated with what is happening in the company. For instance, relationship-specific adaptations may require certain priorities to be made internally. A third type of management problem has to do with the network connections; that is, how to handle the relationship's interdependence with other relationships the company is involved in. Certain actions may, for example, be necessary in order to exploit synergistic effects among relationships or to remove harmful or destructive effects of connections.

It is not possible on the mere basis of the two case studies to elaborate on all aspects of relationship management. Instead, what we shall do is to point to some interesting observations and discuss a few implications that can be drawn from them. The reasoning will be arranged in accordance with the above distinction of three problem areas.

Organization of the technological exchange

The Nippon Steel case offers an interesting example of a collaborative form that is not so common in industrial networks. Together with some ten of its largest customers Nippon Steel has established a company-wide and permanent R&D organization. Figure 6.1 illustrates what the structure may look like. The organization is typically headed by a chairman at the vice-president level. In many cases there is also a small joint steering committee chaired by a person at the director level. Below there are a number of R&D Groups which are responsible for specific product groups such as plate, sheet, pipe, bar and precoated steel. Each such group consists of about thirty people who meet twice a year to exchange information. For example, these meetings can be used to discuss technical problems and to inform each other about new developments. If there is a need to start a joint project, the group can decide to establish a special group consisting of a larger number of representatives of the two companies. The total number of members may amount to forty people, including representatives of various research and testing laboratories and production plants. Sometimes the group is divided into two subgroups – one for R&D and one for production. While the entire group may not meet so often (e.g., once a year), these subgroups meet frequently.

The activity links, resource ties and actor bonds which result from this very long-term and institutionalized interaction have obviously produced a lot of useful results for Nippon Steel, and probably also for their customers. They have made it possible for

```
                        CHAIRMAN
                   (Vice-President level)
                            |
                            |
                            |
                   STEERING COMMITTEE
                     (Director level)
                            |
                            |
        _____
        |                   |                   |
   R&D GROUP 1         R&D GROUP 2         R&D GROUP 3
                            |
                            |_ SPECIAL GROUP ┌─ R&D SUBGROUP
                               (temporary)   └─ PRODUCTION SUBGROUP
                            |
                            ⊢
                            |
                            ⊢
                            |
```

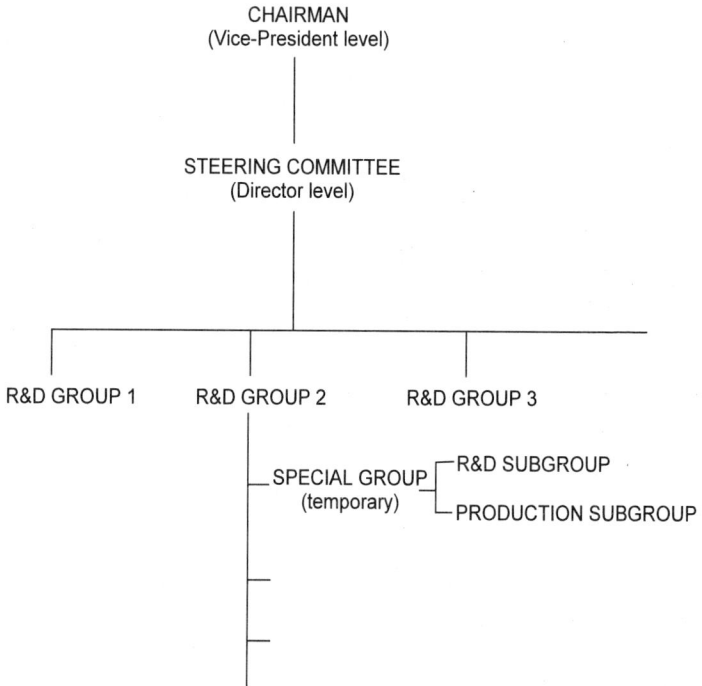

Figure 6.1 Nippon Steel's joint R&D organization with large domestic customers

Nippon Steel to direct its development activities toward the specific needs of these customers. Generally speaking, there is a risk with such a strategy. For example, if the company focuses too much attention on these few relationships there is a risk that it does not become aware of new needs and opportunities arising in other parts of the network. And further, if for some reason its partners become less competitive this might also affect the competitiveness of the supplier. In this particular case, however, these risks do not seem to be overwhelming. The relative maturity of the technology, the stability of the network, and Nippon Steel's strong market position, indicate that this is a viable strategy. Among other things, the big size of Nippon Steel makes it possible to handle a relatively large number of cooperative relationships. A smaller competitor may have to confine itself to fewer partners.

In product areas characterized by a more rapidly changing technology and less stable networks the risks associated with highly formalized and institutionalized arrangements of this type are greater. But at the same time, the need for close technological cooperation with customers or suppliers may be even higher. This is illustrated by the Toshiba case.

The technological exchange between Toshiba and Cummins was originally organized in a more traditional way, by forming a common project group. However, at a later point in time, the partnership was strengthened through the establishment of Enceratec, a jointly owned company. Above all, the role of Enceratec is to commercialize the jointly developed technology in the American market.

The existence of formal structures and formalized communication patterns should not hide the fact that informal interaction plays an important role in almost all technological cooperation. So also in these two cases. However, the formal structure can help to bring individuals together and in that way facilitate the creation of social bonds and the development of a well-functioning communication.

That the informal contacts are important for knowledge creation, one of the three main effects of cooperative relationships, is evident. It has to do, *inter alia*, with the role of tacit knowledge.[6] The organizational process of creating new knowledge, such as novel technology, can be described as a 'spiral' where different modes of knowledge conversion interact (Nonaka, 1991 and 1994; Nonaka and Takeuchi, 1995). The interaction between tacit knowledge and explicit knowledge is particularly important in order to realize the practical benefits of the tacit knowledge held by different individuals. This interaction tends to become larger in scale and faster in speed as more people in and around the organization become involved. Thus, if new knowledge is going to be created at the inter-organizational level, comprising two or several firms, then mutual and dynamic interaction has to be permitted among a larger number of individuals in the organizations concerned. And furthermore, much of this interaction has to be informal if the different knowledge elements are to be effectively used and lead to an upward process of knowledge creation.

It seems that in both of the investigated cases broad and informal contacts, supported by a formal structure, were established between the cooperating companies. This is probably one of the more important reasons why both relationships have been successful from a technology development point of view.

The informal contacts are also important for the activity coordination, another of the three main effects of relationships. In the Toshiba–Cummins cooperation, for example, there were a lot of more or less parallel and interdependent activities that had to be coordinated, functionally as well as in time (process development, parts designing, parts manufacture, parts testing, making and testing of engines, evaluation of test results, cost calculations, etc.). Much of the coordination could certainly be done at the formal meetings. Although the coordination process has not been investigated in detail, it can be assumed on the basis of what is known from other studies that the informal interaction that took place among a large number of people in both companies played an important role for the coordination. Due to technological uncertainties it is usually difficult to work out detailed activity plans in advance. In order to cope with unpredictable events and take the correct action, decentralized measures often have to be taken directly by those who are actually working on the project. In the same way that horizontal communication is important when handling such problems within firms, direct contacts on the operative level are helpful in coordinating activities carried out by two (or several) companies.

It may thus be necessary to establish a broad and informal contact interface on the operative level before a more extensive cooperation can begin to yield fruitful results. But all problems cannot be solved at this level – also illustrated by the Toshiba–Cummins case. In order to solve certain problems which may arise in the cooperation, it is therefore important that there are also good personal relationships at the senior or even top-management levels. The need to have direct access to Toshiba's senior management was strongly felt by Cummins. A specific problem in this context was the frequent job rotation of managers in Toshiba, which meant that this communication channel had to be renewed from time to time.

Another important point, which also has organizational implications, is that the acquisition and use of tacit knowledge requires experience. This means that it is difficult for people to share each other's thinking processes unless there is some form of shared experience to build upon. This holds true within organizations as well as between organizations. Therefore, effective joint knowledge creation cannot take place until the people in the two organizations have worked together for some time and learnt to know each other.

Thanks to the long-term perspective of all actors involved in the two investigated relationships, the people got a chance to build personal ties and acquire the shared experience that paved the way for joint knowledge creation.

Besides the formation of organizational ties, relationships can be formalized and institutionalized through the use of written agreements. Håkansson (1989 and 1990) showed in his study of 123 small and medium-sized Swedish companies (some of which were divisions within larger corporations) that the majority of collaborative relationships were non-formalized in this respect. Instead the relationships were controlled by the use of trust and confidence. He draws the conclusion that formal agreements are not very useful since there are so many parameters and different sources of uncertainty to handle. Formal agreements tend to be used in very special cases, and then primarily as a complement to other control mechanisms.

In both of the present case studies written agreements were in fact used, and, it seems, played more than a marginal role. Both of these cases can be regarded as 'special' since they represent examples of large and strategically important cooperations for the business units involved. Even in countries like Sweden and Japan, where there is no strong tradition to rely extensively on legal contracting (compared with the US for example), written agreements are often considered indispensable in such cases. With regard to Nippon Steel and Toyota the need to have a more extensive contract was not perceived until the project had been running for some time. In this case, and probably in many others, the need for a formal contract is very much linked to the handling of connections with other relationships. One key problem area has to do with the exploitation of the technology outside the relationship in focus. That is an issue that we shall come back to toward the end of this chapter.

Coordination with internal activities and resources

If the technological exchange that takes place with a certain partner is going to produce useful results, it is important that the relationship is well integrated with internal activities. Establishing a broad contact interface is one means to assure such an integration. But as we saw in the Toshiba case, when there are many people involved and the contact pattern is complex, then it is difficult for single individuals to have a full picture of what is going on. This may lead to misunderstandings and friction, both between the parties and within the companies. These frictions may disturb the cooperation and have negative effects on the outcome.

Obviously Cummins' cooperation with Toshiba was not, during a certain period of time, fully anchored in the Cummins organization. The project was run mainly by the Materials Engineering Department. The Engine Development Groups, responsible for developing and testing the engines, were not very cooperative and this caused some problems. It was not until they could be convinced to participate that field testing of the ceramic components could be carried out. The example illustrates the importance of coordinating the technological exchange with internal activities. It also illustrates the importance of using the relationship for resource mobilization. In order to get access to the resources controlled by the Engine Development Groups it was necessary for Toshiba to develop good contacts with them also. If this had not taken place it is possible that the whole project would had failed.

The advantage of having a broad interface of contacts has been emphasized, but the difficulties to control such a relationship have also been pointed out. In order to facilitate the integration with the internal activities, it is known from other research that it might be good to have one or a few persons who are internally responsible for the relationship. This role may be informal, but there might be advantages in formalizing it. This makes the role more visible and gives the holder more authority. In the two case studies there were no formally appointed 'relationship managers'; this kind of coordinating role seems to have been performed informally by several persons. Whether or not this coordinating has functioned well is difficult to say, but at least at Toshiba and Cummins there seem to have been some temporary problems.

An example of formalizing the coordination role can be given from another, ongoing study. In one case that is being investigated, two large companies – one Swedish and one Japanese – are in the process of developing a more far-reaching technological cooperation. After having pursued a more limited cooperation for several years, the Swedish company wished to broaden and deepen the relationship. This decision was followed by a lot of contact-seeking activities by various people in the Swedish company – people who in many cases did not understand how the Japanese company functioned and who lacked knowledge about other exchange activities with the partner. This caused a lot of confusion in the Japanese company, and the situation was described by one person as 'a total mess'. In order to coordinate the communication with the Japanese partner a specific coordinator was appointed. It was a senior manager with long experience of working with Japanese. He describes his role as doing 'the traffic control'. One of his first tasks was to sort out the different internal projects and work out a plan for how each of them should be handled in relation to the partner. Now the channeling of the internal projects is under control, which means that the coordinator can focus his attention on problems concerned with the relationship itself.

Network connections and technology exploitation

Relationships are not isolated dyads in a market. They are integrated entities in a network characterized by a high degree of connectedness. As already has been maintained, the technological exchange that takes place with a certain partner therefore has to be managed in such a way that different existing and potential interdependencies with other relationships are taken into account.

There are of course many types of connections that are relevant for the management of technological exchange.[7] One question is how other relationships can be used for the benefit of a certain customer relationship. For example, are there suppliers to the focal firm who can contribute by adapting or developing their products? We know that the ceramic powder supplied by Toshiba Ceramics is an important raw material for Toshiba's Fine Ceramics Division. To what extent this supplier relationship has affected the Toshiba–Cummins cooperation has not been investigated, however.

At the other end of the production chain, the relationships with the customer's customers or end-users may prove to be useful, or even indispensable, resources. For example, in developing ceramic diesel engine components it was of crucial importance to make field tests. This obviously made it necessary for Cummins to have good relationships with the truck manufacturers and truck owners.

A third type of connection that sometimes requires skillful handling in the context of technology development concerns the relationships with competing customers. For instance, Nippon Steel has parallel cooperative relationships with Toyota and Nissan. In order to be able to maintain trustful and open relationships with both of them, Nippon Steel uses separate teams who are not supposed to exchange information about what they are working on. Of course, this type of organizational solution can only be employed by large companies.[8]

Connections are also important when it comes to exploiting the technology that has been developed within the frame of a business relationship (typically some pieces of technology are the direct result of the knowledge-creating interaction, while others are developed by the individual parties themselves but aimed to be used in the relationship). This is a problem area that concerns both parties, but their interests may be conflicting. There are two interrelated problems concerning the exploitation of the technology outside the focal relationship.

One problem concerns the usage of the developed product by other users. Normally, the manufacturer is interested in continuing the commercialization of the technology by selling the product, or adapted varieties, to other customers. But this is not always in the interest of the partner, since these other customers may be seen as competitors. Here we have a potential conflict that has to be handled. The other problem area concerns the horizontal diffusion of technology to other manufacturers. Here too, there may or may not be conflicting interests as we will see below.

Both of these classical problem situations are well illustrated in the study. Let us first discuss the exploitation of the technology together with other customers. As a matter of fact, it is a common pattern in industrial networks that companies first develop a certain technology or product together with one customer and then sell it to other customers or take it as starting point for developing new products or applications for them. The connection between Matsushita and Toyota is a good example. The development of coated steel sheet for Toyota was initially built on Nippon Steel's previous collaboration with Matsushita, which had resulted in the first commercial application of galvannealed steel in Japan. When a demand for higher corrosion resistance of the autobody appeared, Nippon Steel could use the technology already developed for home appliances together with Matsushita. This transfer was facilitated by the fact that both customers used a similar method to test corrosion-resistance. However, due to technical differences related to the use of the material certain adaptations of the product and the production process were necessary. The close cooperation thereby established subsequently led to the development of a completely new product (i.e., DUREXECELITE). (This product is not of interest to home appliance manufacturers since it is adapted to the specific demands of the automobile industry.)

In this case there was no problem for Nippon Steel to apply the technology developed with Matsushita in the relationship with Toyota. The two customers were not competitors, and moreover Nippon Steel did not depend on intellectual property rights controlled by Matsushita. This connection can thus be characterized as an opportunity rather than a problem.

When it comes to commercializing DUREXCELITE the situation was different. Here we have the not unusual situation, illustrated by Figure 6.2, where a supplier and a customer have jointly developed a new product. The supplier wants to sell the product to other customers who are directly competing with the partner. At the same time, the customer would like to have the possibility to buy the product from other manufacturers, and by this means avoid becoming dependent on one exclusive supplier (this is the

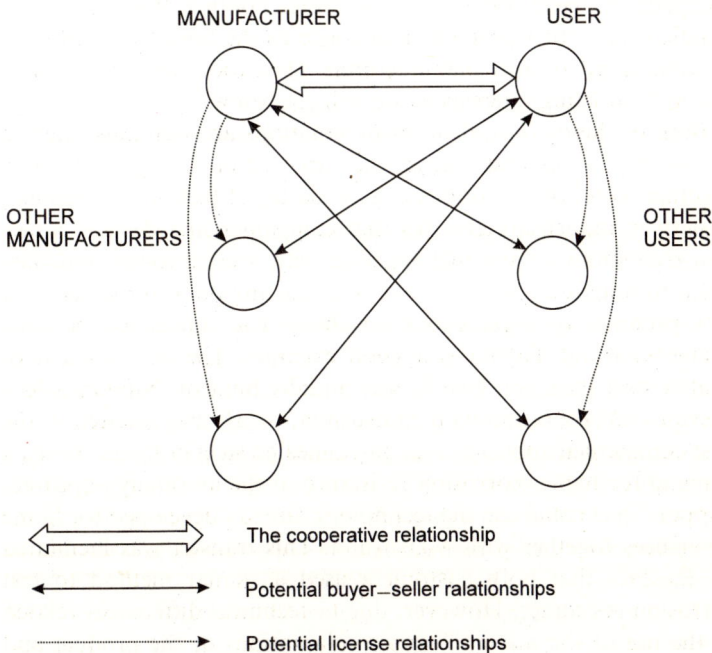

Figure 6.2 The dual problem of exploiting the new technology outside the co-operative relationship

second problem of technology diffusion mentioned above). In this specific case, it was Toyota's policy to have at least two suppliers for each product and it therefore wanted Nippon Steel to license the DUREXCELITE technology to other Japanese steelmakers.

This situation and the potential conflict risk became apparent as the development work proceeded and both parties realized the growing importance of the project – both in terms of resource commitments and commercial potential. It was then decided to make a more comprehensive agreement that regulated, among other things, the conditions under which the two parties could use the research results.

The agreement that was reached after negotiations contained some unique elements compared to what is customary in the steel industry. Although the details cannot be disclosed, it can be said that the agreement meant that the exploitation of the technology for other customers than Toyota was to some extent jointly controlled by the two companies (the normal practice is that the manufacturing-related patents are owned by the steelmaker and the application-related patents by the user, and that they are both free to use their own patents as they wish).

An effect of such an agreement must be to reduce the producer's freedom of action as to the marketing of the new product. Therefore, one can guess that the decision to share the technology with Toyota was preceded by some internal discussions within Nippon Steel. It is true that the original invention of the new coating concept had been made by one of its engineers, and some people could certainly find arguments why the total control of the product technology should stay with Nippon Steel. However, these arguments had to be weighed against the facts that Toyota had not only made important contributions to the development of the technology but also happened to be Nippon Steel's largest customer. The relationship with Toyota was extremely important both from an economic and a development point of view and could not be treated as any other customer relationship. It seems that the agreement that was finally reached was designed in such a way as to satisfy the long-term interests of both companies.

The second issue, i.e. the licensing of 'the DUREXCELITE technology' to other steelmakers, was obviously easier to solve. The solution was to let the competitors buy a license, but only after one and a half years, a period during which Nippon Steel was allowed to make all deliveries to Toyota. This practice of granting licenses to each other is common among the five big steelmakers in Japan. It is partly a consequence of the purchasing policies pursued by the large steel consumers such as Toyota and the other auto-makers. This policy aims at preserving the balance among these producers. Although these buyers have established close relation-ships with the steelmakers, in order to make the exchange more efficient they are at the same time consciously acting in a way that stimulates competition. Forcing the suppliers to license technology to their competitors is one ingredient in this policy. This is prob-ably one of the reasons why it is so difficult for Japanese steel-makers to increase their market shares in Japan.[9] Obviously, Nippon Steel holds an open attitude toward the sharing of propri-etary technology with its competitors. The same can be said about Toshiba. Like Nippon Steel it realizes that transferring technology that enables other producers to enter the market helps to speed up the market growth rate. This is easy to understand from a network point of view. As long as there is only one producer of a new, revolutionary product many potential customers and other actors concerned are hesitant to make the necessary adaptations. But if there are several competing suppliers investing in the same technol-ogy, the perceived risk of investing their own resources will be less. There is a greater chance that the new product will remain on the market and be further improved. And moreover, the buyers know that they will not become totally dependent on a single producer's future capability and policy.

So there may in fact be marketing reasons for the innovator to share the technology with others. But that is not the only conceiv-able reason. If the new technology represents a major break-through and the potential market is big, then the innovating firm knows that it may be difficult to stop the diffusion of the technol-ogy in the long run. No matter how strong the patent, competitors will always find ways to enter the market sooner or later. Instead of the innovator keeping the technology within the company it may be better to spread it in a controlled way. By doing so, money can be made on the licensing business and, probably more impor-tant, the innovator can control the diffusion and the continued technological development in a direction that is favorable. For example, if the innovator's technology can be made the industry standard, this will probably help the innovator to take a larger share of the market and increase the chance of remaining a tech-nological leader.

Even if there are advantages with technology sharing, this does not mean that all proprietary technology should automatically be licensed out. The advantages must of course be weighed against the negative effects on the company's competitiveness. There are several questions that have to be addressed by the innovating firm. For example, what parts of the technology should be made available? Who should be allowed to buy? And what is the appropriate timing? The answers depend on situation-specific factors which have to be carefully analyzed – by using a network approach for example.

As is illustrated by the Nippon Steel case, the outcome may be a compromise between the interests of the partners who have developed the technology. Nippon Steel had to give its competitors the right to produce the new product, but the transfer was delayed and the patent rights were not accompanied by any production know-how. That gave Nippon Steel a chance to keep ahead of the competition. If we take the other case, Toshiba only licensed some specific, but critical, parts of its sintering technology. This was done at an early stage to enable certain other producers to make a dense material and thereby to help Toshiba develop the market. The results of the subsequent product- and application-oriented development work carried out in cooperation with Cummins have not been licensed. In this case there is no pressure from the customer to make the technology available to other producers. Instead the two companies have joined forces to continue the commercialization of the technology (this was facilitated by the fact that Cummins had established a separate business area for components).

Chapter 7

A concluding note on the interacting and networking behavior of Japanese companies

The analysis of the two cases has revealed that there are many similarities between the interacting and networking behavior observed in Toshiba and Nippon Steel and in the kind of patterns found in other studies of technological innovation. This did not come as a big surprise. The same type of fundamental dependencies and heterogeneities characterize Japanese networks as much as industrial networks in other parts of the world. Moreover, many Japanese companies are operating in networks that are highly internationalized. Furthermore, technology development is as uncertain in Japan as elsewhere. Therefore, it is logical that Japanese companies encounter the same type of difficulties in developing and commercializing new industrial products as companies based in other countries. In order to overcome various barriers and to handle uncertainties they need to relate their own resources and activities to those of other actors in the environment. For example, in order to develop practical applications, a critical phase in all product development, they have to find partners (customers/users) with whom they can do that and establish cooperative relationships with them. Like companies from other countries, the identity of their partners is of great importance since it determines in what directions the company's capabilities and competitive advantages are moving. Managing the technological exchange, in relation to the network as a whole as well as with regard to individual relationships, is consequently as necessary and challenging for Japanese companies as it is for other types of firms.

But the recognition of these fundamental similarities does not mean that there cannot be systematic international differences with regard to *how* companies manage the innovation process – for example, to what extent they rely on external resources;

what type of cooperative relationships they prefer; how they select their partners; and how they try to control and manage the relationships. An interesting question is thus if there are any significant differences in how Japanese companies use relationships in technological development compared with companies from other parts of the world, for example Western Europe or North America.

Let me first make it clear, though, that I do not believe that there is only one Japanese approach to technological cooperation. Needless to say, there is variation among Japanese companies in the same way as there are differences among firms from other countries. None the less, it cannot be ruled out that certain typically Japanese patterns of interacting and networking behavior exist. Such distinguishing characteristics could, for example, be explained by the unique features of the Japanese environment. As emphasized by many observers the Japanese business practices differ from those in the West due to different historical pasts and cultural backgrounds.

There are of course many factors that affect how Japanese, as well as other, companies interact with other actors in the environment. As illustrated in Figure 7.1, roughly speaking we can distinguish between two main groups of influencing factors. One is concerned with the characteristics of the industrial system to which the company belongs. The other group consists of company-related factors. Needless to say, the two types of factors are not independent of each other. What individual companies look like and how they function is to a large extent the result of the environment. At the same time, the industrial system is shaped by the actions of the companies and other organizations that make up the system. At least two types of underlying factors contribute to shape the industrial system and the companies: the national culture, and other characteristics of the country and society in question. Also these two groups of factors are interdependent.

It would carry us too far from the purpose of this study to describe in a complete way what characterizes the Japanese industrial system and the Japanese company. Instead, some widely acknowledged characteristics will first be mentioned. After that it will be discussed, somewhat tentatively, how some of these factors might affect the Japanese companies' way of interacting in connection with technology development. Let us start with the industrial system and later on proceed to the firm.

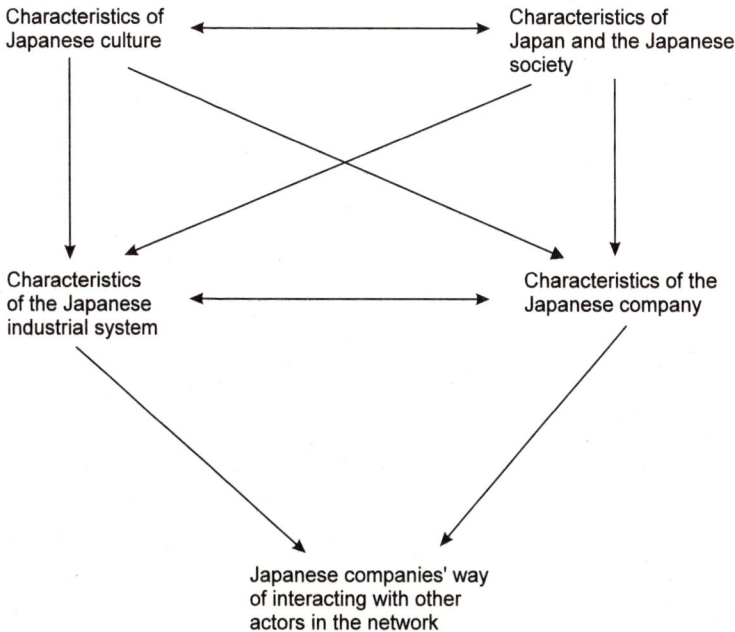

Figure 7.1 Groups of factors influencing the interaction and networking behavior of Japanese companies

7.1 THE JAPANESE INDUSTRIAL SYSTEM AND TECHNOLOGICAL COOPERATION

The term 'industrial system' is here used in a broad sense. It embraces not only the total industrial network, as defined by the theoretical framework, but also other relevant parts of the society and its institutions. It can be argued that the following characteristics are distinctive for the Japanese industrial system:

- The importance of long-term relationships and business groupings (*keiretsu*).
- Strong rivalry in many (but not all) domestic markets.
- Demanding customers.
- Relatively low degree of vertical integration in many companies.
- A comparatively large number of small and medium-sized companies.

- A complex distribution system which is difficult and costly to access for those who are outside.
- A unique labor market which is characterized, for example, by the practice of lifetime employment in certain companies.
- The existence of strong social networks among politicians, businessmen, and bureaucrats.
- An active industrial policy.

As is easily recognized some dependencies exist among these factors. For example, the existence of close inter-firm relationships within the business groups makes it easier and less risky for individual member companies to pursue a high degree of vertical specialization. Probably this kind of behavior also contributes to explain why the Japanese industrial system is characterized by such a large share of small and medium-sized companies. Furthermore, the complexity and inaccessibility of the distribution system can partly be explained by the existence of vertically organized systems of distributors which operate under the name of a large-scale manufacturer.

Let us now briefly discuss, against the background of the two case studies, how some of these factors may influence the Japanese company's way of interacting with others in the context of technological development.

Keiretsu and social networks

The existence of institutionalized groupings of affiliated and cooperating companies in Japan – *keiretsu* as they are often called, especially by non-Japanese writers – is a topic which has attracted a tremendous amount of interest in recent years.[1] There are several types of such enterprise groupings. One is the large-scale 'financial', 'horizontal' or 'intermarket' *keiretsu* which consist of diversified groups which can be likened to core members, consisting of a commercial bank (with other affiliated financial institutions) and a general trading house (*sogo shosha*), which are surrounded by a range of large manufacturing firms representing a highly diversified set of industries and markets. There are six such major intermarket *keiretsu*: the modern descendants of the prewar *zaibatsu*, i.e. Mitsui, Mitsubishi and Sumitomo, and the three big bank-centered groups, i.e. Fuji, Sanwa and Dai-Ichi Kangyo. These groupings can be characterized as being loosely coupled, network-type inter-firm alliances which are kept together through mutual shareholding, bank borrowing, interlocking directorship, membership in the group's presidents' council, and to a lesser extent intermediate product trade (Gerlach, 1992b).

'Vertical' or 'industrial' *keiretsu* is another major type of Japanese grouping. They consist of large manufacturing companies (such as members of the above-mentioned intermarket *keiretsu*) and their affiliated upstream suppliers and downstream distributors. The parent companies typically have 300–500 such satellite companies in related industries which are tightly and hierarchically tied to the former through long-term business relationships and, in some cases, partial ownership. The long-run exchange in such cooperative vertical relationships not only includes an economic component but also one in which trust, loyalty and power are transacted as well (Imai, 1989).

Both types of *keiretsu* have been seen as sources of Japanese competitive advantages and rapid growth, although considerable disagreement has emerged over the nature of the *keiretsu* and their significance to the Japanese economy (Gerlach, 1992a). With regard to the intermarket *keiretsu* especially, there are divergent opinions regarding their relevance to understanding the Japanese industrial system. According to one view, often put forward by Japanese, these groupings have only a social function and the membership in a certain *keiretsu* has no real impact on the company's actual business. Several Japanese managers whom I met during the research explicitly denied the importance (almost the existence) of the intermarket *keiretsu*. This view has been questioned by foreign observers who argue that preferential trading among *keiretsu* affiliates is a reality in the contemporary Japanese economy and that transactions in equity and debt capital are especially important (Gerlach, 1992a).

So, what is the importance of *keiretsu* to technological innovation and inter-firm cooperation? With regard to the intermarket *keiretsu*, opinions are divided as indicated above. However, as maintained by several scholars the existence of this type of *keiretsu* affects Japanese companies' willingness and ability to invest in long-term and risky R&D projects thanks to such *keiretsu* features as ownership dominated by 'friendly' shareholders belonging to the same group; the access to a 'mini capital market' within the group that facilitates R&D financing and protects the firm from the pressures for short-term return of normal capital markets; and the intensive information exchange that is fostered by the sense of kinship felt among member companies (see, e.g., Makino, 1992; Ballon, 1992; Nakatani, 1990; Gerlach, 1992a).[2]

It seems reasonable to believe that intermarket *keiretsu* membership has at least some importance for companies' innovative activities. But the literature says very little about to what extent these activities are carried out in the form of intra-*keiretsu* cooperation, and how the intra-*keiretsu* collaborative relationships look like and possibly differ from other collaborative relationships. Some evidence of group-wide technology projects exist. Gerlach (1992b, pp. 149–55) briefly describes some intra-*keiretsu* joint projects, such as for example the Mitsubishi C&C Kenkyu-kai. This study group was formed in 1981 and brought together forty Mitsubishi companies to develop technologies relating to high-level data transmission. But as pointed out by Gerlach such joint projects often appear to be symbolic and more important for establishing the position of the group within the larger business community than for pursuing their immediate economic interests (*ibid.*, p. 150). Moreover, Kodama (1986 and 1992) has suggested that a key advantage of the Japanese enterprise groupings may be that they enable 'fusion innovation' that cuts across several industrial sectors. However, good empirical descriptions of the intra-*keiretsu* technology cooperation seem to missing.

The present study touches upon the issue in the Toshiba case. While Nippon Steel is a 'non-*keiretsu* firm', Toshiba is a member of the Mitsui group. However, there is nothing in the case that indicates that Toshiba's relationships with other Mitsui companies have had any impact on the development of structural ceramics. It is known that Toyota, which is also a member of Mitsui (but considered to be relatively independent), at one point in time was looking for partners for the development of ceramic engine components. Obviously, the contacts which occurred between Toshiba and Toyota did not lead to any cooperation in this field. This is just one episode, so it is not possible to draw any conclusions regarding the importance of *keiretsu* affiliation from that observation. The question of how the intermarket *keiretsu* affects the selection of R&D partners and the content and form of cooperative relationships still remains to be addressed.

When it comes to the vertical *keiretsu*, their positive role in fostering technological innovation is more unanimously recognized. It is a well-known fact that major industrial companies in the Japanese automobile, electrical appliances and other engineering industries carry out much of their trade with affiliated vertically linked suppliers and distributors. In the case of the automobile industry, for example, 'a dominant portion of parts obtained from outside the company is purchased from firms with which the core firm has long-standing relations' (Asanuma, 1989, p. 5). The close, stable and trustful relationships between assemblers and their subcontractors are, *inter alia*, used to get the suppliers actively involved at an early stage in the product development and to exchange proprietary, sometimes tacit, technical and market knowledge – functions that contribute to make the innovation process more efficient and effective (see, e.g., Nakatani, 1990; Makino, 1992; Harryson, 1995). As pointed out by Nakatani (1990), the vertical *keiretsu* play a different role for the technological development than the horizontal ones:

> the horizontal affiliation of firms is useful for exchange of information concerning products and technological progress in different areas and ultimately for technology fusion and development of new technology. The vertical affiliation of firms is more useful in the refinement and customization of existing products and in the development of new products based on close consultation between the core firm and subcontractors in the earliest stages of product development.
>
> (Nakatani, 1990, p. 158)

Due to its large size, power and capability, Nippon Steel cannot be regarded as a 'normal' subcontractor to Toyota. Yet its long-lasting cooperation with this customer can be seen as an example of the kind of close technological exchange that exists within vertical *keiretsu* relationships in Japan. As pointed out when commenting on the case, this type of supplier–customer interaction also exists in the West, but in Japan the cooperative relationships are probably more common and more systematically developed and used. In other words, there are reasons to believe that Japanese manufacturing companies, more often than their Western counterparts, have recognized the potential benefits of developing close cooperative relationships with their suppliers and customers and utilizing these relationships for technological development. As described by Imai *et al.* (1988, pp. 551–8) leading Japanese companies use hierarchically designed 'supplier networks' to speed up the new product development process. These networks are characterized by a shared division of labor, risk and responsibility that facilitates collective innovation in a similar way as internal cross-functional development teams.

Based on empirical data, Tselichtchev (1994) argues that the importance of vertical R&D cooperation in the Japanese industry is in fact increasing. He means that the current trend is to move interaction between core manufacturers and subcontractors toward more innovative activities. In order to exploit synergies the core companies tend to concentrate purchases on the most efficient suppliers, which are entrusted with larger responsibility for product development and component design. At the same time the buying firms are becoming more deeply involved with what is happening in the supplier firms and assist them in various ways in order to increase their technological potential. But the initiative to strengthen supplier–customer linkages based on joint innovative activities comes not only from the buying side. Also the subcontractors themselves are making efforts to enhance their innovative capabilities as a means to increase their bargaining power and change the traditional, hierarchical subcontracting system built on the core firms' 'dictatorial' power over suppliers.[3] Although Nippon Steel is not a subcontractor, it can be maintained that its establishment of closer technological cooperation with key customers since the early 1980s is in line with the general trend.

It should be noted that the importance of long-term and trustful relationships is not limited to the formalized *keiretsu* (this is illustrated by the Nippon Steel case for example). In fact, the entire Japanese industrial system can be viewed as an interconnected network of inter-firm relationships. Principally, this is no different from how the corresponding industrial markets are organized in Western Europe.[4] The main difference is that the Japanese networks tend to be relatively more tightly knit and, moreover, are formalized to a larger degree. It is not only the intermarket *keiretsu* which are formalized through their presidents' councils and by other means. The vertical *keiretsu* use a similar coordination mechanism in the form of special supplier associations (*kyoryokukai*), which bring together the managements of the assembling firms and their first-tier suppliers (Gerlach, 1992c, pp. 8–9).

Various authors have described how *keiretsu* relationships were once formed as a response to the threat of foreign acquisitions and foreign competition. Imai (1989), for example, argues that Japanese companies were in fact forced to cooperate with outside suppliers during the post-war period in order to cope with the severe competitive environment. The companies then discovered, through learning by doing, that close supplier–customer linkages were effective and enabled them to perform dynamic adaptation when market conditions changed. But besides this 'rational' explanation, there are certainly cultural explanations why the Japanese are so prone to build industrial networks. It is a well-known fact that Japanese society is characterized by strong group orientation and high appreciation of personal relations based on trust. It is probable that these traits not only mark the interaction within social groups and organizations but also the interaction that takes place between firms that are mutually dependent on each other. Thus, Japanese firms, or rather their managers and personnel, probably have a more natural inclination to value and develop long-term cooperative relationships with their business partners than Western firms for example.

An issue related to the *keiretsu* one is the existence of social networks and their importance to the functioning of the Japanese industrial system. *Jinmyaku* is the Japanese word used to denote the kind of personal relations that exist among Japanese businessmen, bureaucrats and politicians, and which are continually exploited for the preferment or protection of individual and group interests (van Wolferen, 1989). *Jinmyaku* are considered to be crucial to life in Japan at all levels of the society, and the business world is no exception. *Jinmyaku* thus constitute a vital force for shaping the business landscape for Japanese companies in Japan as well as outside (Holden, 1991).

The role of such personal relations has not been investigated in the present study. Generally speaking, however, it can be expected that the social networks existing across organizational and *keiretsu* borders are important to the technology development. They can, for example, be used to transmit information among companies, between companies and research institutions, and between companies and governmental agencies. It occurs through informal contacts and through all those 'study groups' (*benkyo-kai* and *kenkyu-kai*) that are so popular in Japan.

Demanding customers

That the Japanese buyer is a demanding customer and that this affects the behavior of selling firms is widely recognized. Every visitor to Japan notices how eager the Japanese vendors of goods and services are to satisfy the wishes of their clients. That Japanese industrial buyers are also extremely demanding and have to be treated 'like kings' can be confirmed by practically every foreign company that has entered the Japanese market.

There are probably several reasons why the Japanese customers are so demanding. One is the intensive competitive environment (created by the concentration of a very large population in a small geographical area), which offers the buyers many choices and 'spoils' them. But here too, there are probably some culturally contingent factors as well. The Japanese have long been known to appreciate neatness and precision. They like things that are clean, proper and perfect. This attitude affects their buying behavior both as consumers and as professional purchasers.

It is probable that this culturally rooted behavior, in combination with the competitive environment, contributes to the emergence of close supplier–customer relationships in industrial markets. In order to meet the requirements of important customers, the sellers often have to engage in technological development with these customers, who are themselves active buyers. The Nippon Steel case is a good illustration.

That Japanese customers are often more active and demand a more intensive technological exchange than other customers is recognized by many foreign companies. Several Swedish firms which have been interviewed in other contexts say that Japanese customers are always interested in new products, but that it takes longer, when compared to customers in other markets, to convince them of the product's merits. There are so many detailed questions that have to be answered. One specialty metals producer describes how its Japanese customers often take the initiative to involve the supplier in applications development. These projects often go on for several years and give the supplier valuable knowledge that can be exploited not only in Japan but outside also. 'As an engineer it is enjoyable to work with the Japanese, since they are so demanding and technically qualified,' the technical director says. He also says that more recently this type of technological cooperation has spread to other markets. Many German and American customers in particular have learned how to work with their suppliers in a more long-term way.

One effect of Japanese customers' purchasing behavior is that suppliers have to adapt their products to individual customer requirements more often than they need to do in other countries. There is a widespread preference among Japanese companies to have their own systems. For example, a large computer manufacturer has been forced to develop different computer systems for every bank in Japan. It is impossible to persuade a customer to use the same system as another competing bank. To meet these demands the supplier has to cooperate with each bank (a comparison is Nippon Steel's development of different coatings for different automobile manufacturers). In the US, where the company is also selling bank systems, it can use a more standardized solution. This substantially reduces the product development costs compared with the Japanese market.

Active industrial policy

The role and importance of the Japanese industrial policy in the post-war era have been extensively researched. Although there is some disagreement on how important it has been for the competitiveness of the Japanese industry, especially in the recent decades, it is a fact that the Japanese government, more than governments in many other countries, has actively tried to influence industry – not least in the area of science and technology. One of the policy instruments employed by the government is various types of national programs. MITI's Fine Ceramics Program briefly described in the Toshiba case is one example.

These national programs are seen as a means to promote technology development through joint action among companies and public research institutions. However, although the specified targets may be expressed in technical terms, the ultimate goal is always to achieve commercialization and economic development. An important and explicit aim of many programs is therefore to establish cooperation between various actors. In the case of fine ceramics, for instance, MITI believed in the importance of bringing manufacturers and users closer together in order to pave the way for commercial applications. This goal influenced MITI in its selection of participating companies. In the case of Toshiba there were no concrete effects of the program in this regard. On the whole, there seems to have been few supplier–customer cooperations within the program itself so far. According to MITI officials this can be explained by the early stage of the technology development (Laage-Hellman, 1991). But the contacts established through the program are expected to remain after the program has been finished and to trigger more application-oriented joint R&D in the future.

It is true that national R&D programs also exist in other countries, such as in the US and several West European countries (sometimes with Japan as a model). However, it seems that such programs are more extensively used in Japan than elsewhere. Moreover, it is the author's impression that the role of the programs in promoting network formation (besides the direct knowledge creation) is also more consciously used in Japan. In Japan the programs, and other contact-building activities, are seen as tools for the government to support the creation of an industrial structure with high innovation propensity.

It should be pointed out that the government's efforts to support cooperation among companies are not made at the expense of competition in the marketplace. On the contrary, it is a conscious policy of the Japanese government to act in such a way as to preserve competition among the different manufacturers.

7.2 THE JAPANESE COMPANY AND TECHNOLOGICAL COOPERATION

There is an abundant literature on the organization and management of Japanese companies. Among those many features that are often claimed to characterize the large Japanese company, the following ones can be expected to have some impact on the way R&D and commercialization activities are carried out:

- A consensus-seeking decision-making process (including such phenomena as *nemawashi* and *ringi*).
- An incremental planning process, which emphasizes long-term visions and short-term action plans rather than the development of a 'grand strategy'.
- An organization built on the principles of redundancy, hierarchy, internal competition, informal contact networks, and teamwork.
- Passive owners who normally do not interfere in the management of the company.
- A unique human resource management system based on lifetime employment (for certain categories of employees), seniority based promotion, extensive job rotation and in-house training, and strong company culture.

- Strategies that give priority to long-term survival and growth (rather than short-term profitability), and include the following types of element: longsightedness, continuous improvements in all fields (*kaizen*), high market shares, manufacturing excellence and high quality, intensive product development, internal diversification, and high debt–equity ratio.
- Effective use of external resources through establishment of cooperative relationships with business partners (rather than doing everything in-house).

It has not been possible to cover all of these features in the two case studies. Here, the discussion will therefore be confined to just a few selected aspects that are highlighted in the study.

The issue of external resource utilization, which is also coupled to the characteristics of the industrial system, has already been discussed and will therefore not be explicitly dealt with in this section.

Longsightedness

Both cases give evidence of the longsightedness and perseverance which characterize the strategy of many Japanese companies. Toshiba's and Nippon Steel's long-term commitment to the development of structural fine ceramics and coated steel sheet respectively is clearly reflected in the way they interact with the environment. Nippon Steel, operating in a relatively stable network, has gone so far as to make permanent and institutionalize the technological cooperation with its most important customers in the automobile industry.[5] The development and improvement of the coated steel is seen as an endless process which requires a continuous interaction with the users. It is true that the Nippon Steel case is unique, in terms of the broad and institutionalized form of cooperation with customers, but the other major Japanese steelmakers also have long-term relationships and technological exchange with the automobile companies.

Toshiba's approach to the development of silicon nitride is extremely long term. The basic research began thirty years ago. More applied and commercially oriented R&D work has been going on for over fifteen years and still the real breakthrough in the market-place remains to be made. Obviously, Toshiba's investments in this field have not been governed by expectations for a short-term financial return, but a belief in the strategic importance of this technology. Toshiba's tenacious efforts put into the search for suitable partners and developing cooperative relationships with selected users have been an important element of the emerging development strategy in the field of structural ceramics.

Toshiba was not the only Japanese ceramics manufacturer to pursue such a strategy. It can be mentioned that several others, such as Kyocera, NGK Spark Plug and Asahi Glass, were also quite active in establishing early joint development and tie-ups with users.[6] This was considered necessary in order to reap the advantages of their original technology (Kimura, 1985, p. 23). In the case of NGK Spark Plug the research on silicon nitride began in the 1960s, while the first application was not realized until 1985 (after several years of close cooperation with Nissan). Obviously, this company has also demonstrated a remarkable patience and perseverance.

The strategies of the American and European manufacturers and users have not been investigated. However, it is well known that leading US companies such as Norton, Ford Motor, Westinghouse and Garrett were deeply involved in close cooperation with each other as well as with some Japanese ceramics manufacturers in the 1970s and 1980s. The fact that Norton, in spite of an early technical lead in silicon nitride technology, came to lag behind the Japanese in developing and implementing commercial applications might (possibly) be explained by a less long-term and persevering strategy.

Teamwork approach

The concept of teamwork primarily has to do with how a company organizes its own development activities,[7] but it also has some relevance for the external exchange. On the whole, when it comes to large diversified corporations like Toshiba it may be difficult to define what is to be considered as internal exchange and external exchange respectively. Some business units may be operating very independently, and their way of interacting with other business units within the parent company and its group may be rather similar to how they interact with other companies. As described by Campbell (1991, p. 3) large Japanese companies can be said to operate a kind of borderless network where 'there is little difference in the relationships between organizational units which are hundred percent owned, those which are partially owned and those which are legally fully independent'. In other words, there is no clear boundary between the company and its environment. The Japanese large companies can thus be described as an interorganizational network of internal and external relationships. 'These relationships are characterized by information sharing, diffused authority, long-term personal relationships, and a combination and control of cooperation and competition between network members' (*ibid.*, p. 7).

The present study suggests that this deliberately created internal network, embedded in an external network of relationships with customers, suppliers and so on, effectively stimulates and facilitates a teamwork approach to technological innovation. The existence of teamwork is clearly evident in the Toshiba case. It is true that the early development of silicon nitride technology was strongly dependent on Dr Komeya's and his colleagues' pioneering research, carried out within an organization which allowed a lot of personal freedom to individual scientists.[8] But there is no doubt that the frequent interaction among different research groups within the R&D Center had crucial importance for the key discovery of yttria as an efficient sintering aid.[9] Later on, during the applied research and development phase, the Metal Products/Fine Ceramics Division's development of silicon nitride components was actively supported by several other units within Toshiba. Figure 7.2 shows some of the more important Toshiba units with which the division had a more or less intensive information exchange or cooperation.

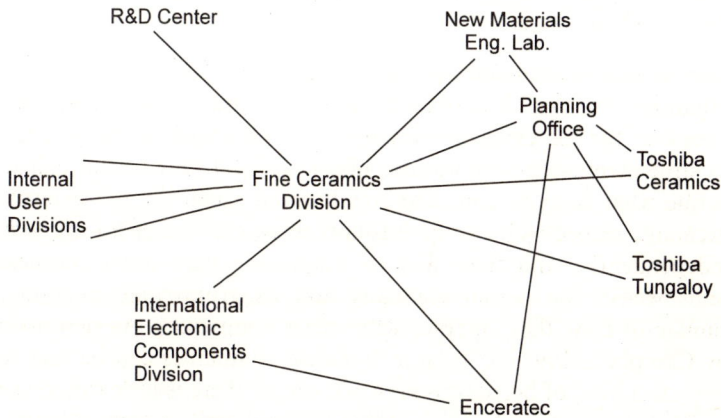

Figure 7.2 Different Toshiba units involved in the development of silicon nitride components

They were all working toward the same long-term goal, for which they had a shared (but not explicitly stated) responsibility, but contributed in different ways according to their respective competencies and roles. The activities of the different organizational units, comprising research and development as well as marketing and production, were not (primarily) controlled through hierarchy. Instead the coordination was to a large extent horizontal and based on relational norms resulting from social ties, trust, shared values, and solidarity.[10] The mutual interdependence and close relationships created strong incentives to support each other and to seek cooperative solutions together.

Admitting the existence of variation among Japanese as well as non-Japanese companies, it is suggested that a teamwork approach may be more common in Japanese large companies than in their Western counterparts. In my belief Western companies' approach to technological innovation is more often individualistic. There tends to be more competition and emphasis on individual contribution. We can take Cummins as an example. The development of the adiabatic engine was very much the work of one man, Dr Kamo. The project was not integrated with other activities in the company and did not receive full support from other internal units (it seems in fact as if Dr Kamo was more successful in establishing relationships with and getting support from various external actors). Also, in the subsequent project on wear parts a real team effort seems to have been missing. Obviously the objective to develop ceramic components for the conventional engine was not shared by all parties concerned, and this made it difficult to obtain the support needed from other organizational units.

But as hinted at above, the teamwork approach is certainly not unique to Japan. It has for example been described by interviewees how the early government-sponsored US efforts to develop silicon nitride technology in the 1970s were characterized by an interdisciplinary team approach. A team effect was achieved by, among other means, forming a network of cooperating companies and laboratories representing different complementary competencies, including manufacturing, design and usage of ceramic components.

Redundancy and phase overlapping

Many successful Japanese companies have gained distinction for their ability to respond quickly to customer needs, create new markets, rapidly develop new products, and dominate emergent technologies. As explained by Nonaka (1991) the secret of their success can to a large measure be attributed to the unique Japanese approach to managing the creation of new knowledge. In discussing the organizational design behind this approach the importance of building a redundant organization is emphasized. Redundancy – that is the conscious overlapping of company information, business activities, and managerial responsibilities – is important because it encourages frequent dialogue and communication and helps to create a 'common cognitive ground' among team members. It facilitates the articulation and internalization of tacit knowledge,[11] which are critical stages in the dynamic knowledge spiral through which the company's technology base grows.

There are several ways to build redundancy into the organization, such as adoption of an overlapping approach, internal competition, job rotation, and providing wide access to company information (Nonaka, 1994). Conscious phase overlapping is an important tool used by Japanese companies to manage the innovation process (see, e.g., Imai, 1989; Takeuchi and Nonaka, 1986). The approach, sometimes described as a rugby game, is used instead of the traditional, sequential and relay-type approach under which a product development project moves in a step-wise fashion from phase to phase (e.g., conceptualization, designing, feasibility testing, development, pilot production, final production, distribution, and marketing). Under 'the Japanese' approach the product development process emerges from the constant interaction and information sharing among various actors concerned with the project, and as a result the different phases come to overlap each other considerably.

The internal processes of knowledge creation have not been investigated in detail. However, it seems that both Toshiba and Nippon Steel have demonstrated an ability to create new knowledge and innovations by making tacit knowledge and insights of individual employees available for testing and use by others in the organization. Moreover, it seems that this dynamic spreading and utilization of tacit knowledge extends beyond the boundary of the companies. Both of the focal companies tried to involve potential users at an early stage. The result was an effective overlapping of different phases which created a shared division of labor among the participating companies and contributed to increase the speed and flexibility of the development process. For example, in the case of

Nippon Steel a redundant joint organization was formed with Toyota, and this contributed to establish a common sense of direction and facilitated the diffusion of tacit knowledge. Since representatives of the cooperating companies shared overlapping information and responsibilities, they could understand what others were struggling to articulate. Among other effects, this helped to mobilize commitment (i.e., a collective sense of identity with the project) and the embodying of tacit knowledge from both partners in the new products. It can be recalled that the information flow in the individual cooperative relationships was so open that it became necessary for Nippon Steel to isolate from each other those teams who were working with different customers – this in order to eliminate the risk of confidential information leaking from one customer to another.

It can of course be questioned to what extent this overlapping approach is unique or particularly typical of Japanese companies and why it appeared in Japan. Imai (1989), focusing primarily on the interaction with outside suppliers rather than customers, argues that Japanese companies were forced to adopt this method during the postwar period in response to severe competition from foreign competitors. The possibility of phase overlapping was thus one of the effects of developing close supplier relationships (cf. the *keiretsu* discussion above). In the same way as companies learned through experience that close and stable relationships with suppliers paid off, they may have learned that close relationships were also valuable on the customer side. Nippon Steel's current policy of establishing institutionalized R&D relationships with large customers was based on the good experience of the first attempts made in the late 1970s.

If we accept that the Japanese were pioneers in using phase overlapping to manage the innovation process, it is now clear that they are no longer the only ones doing that. Many Western firms, some of which were once outperformed by Japanese rivals, have tried to learn the Japanese approach and implemented such methods as simultaneous engineering, cross-functional teams, and close technological cooperation with business partners. The degree of success seems to vary, however, and this probably has to do with the extent to which the Western companies manage to create the type of organizational redundancy that can be found within leading Japanese companies. Redundancy plays a key role in the knowledge creation process, but may sound unappealing to many Western managers since it has a connotation of unnecessary duplication and waste of resources (Nonaka, 1994). It is true that redundant information provides a vehicle for new product development that follows procedures that are different from those specified by the formal organization. But redundancy makes the interchange between hierarchy and non-hierarchy more effective in problem solving and knowledge creation and enables all members of the organization (internal or joint) to participate in the process on the basis of consensus and equal preparation.

Notes

1 INTRODUCTION

1 By the term 'industrial products' we mean goods and services which are used by firms or organizations as input to their own operations (e.g., manufacturing or distribution). Raw or processed materials, components, and production equipment can be mentioned as three important categories of industrial goods (Håkansson, 1982b, pp. 34–5).

2 In a more recent study, it has been concluded that relationships between makers and users of machine tools are weaker in the US than in other countries. This is said to be a key contributor to the decline of the American machine-tool industry and the users' own lack of competitiveness in international markets (Dertouzos et al., 1989, p. 100).

2 TECHNOLOGICAL DEVELOPMENT IN INDUSTRIAL MARKETS

1 This model is more thoroughly described in Laage-Hellman (1989, Ch. 3). It is a further development of an earlier model for analyzing buyer–seller relationships from a marketing and purchasing point of view (Håkansson, 1982b, Ch. 2).

2 This is said to characterize the Japanese society (Campbell et al., 1990, Appendix 2).

3 This section is based on Håkansson and Snehota (1995, Ch. 2).

4 Håkansson's (1989 and 1990) cross-sectional study of 123 Swedish industrial firms addresses these questions more explicitly and describes at an aggregated level the patterns of external collaboration that characterize these companies. By relating the observed collaborative modes to variables describing other dimensions of corporate behavior and its environment, Håkansson draws a number of conclusions about how companies handle their technological development in relation to external firms and organizations.

3 METHODOLOGY

1 There are reasons to believe that differences between individual companies' behavior within a country are at least as great as differences between countries.

4 DEVELOPMENT AND COMMERCIALIZATION OF Zn–Fe ALLOY COATED STEEL SHEET FOR AUTOBODIES

1 In Håkansson (1987a) the term 'mummify' is used to name this type of behavior. Waluszewski's (1989) study of the emergence of a new pulp-making technology gives several examples of equipment and knowledge that were reevaluated when it was discovered that they could be combined with other resources not available previously.

5 DEVELOPMENT AND COMMERCIALIZATION OF STRUCTURAL FINE CERAMICS

1 'Fine ceramics' is the English term customarily used in Japan. 'Advanced ceramics' and 'engineering ceramics' are other common terms used to denote the same class of materials.
2 In connection with the hundred-year anniversary of the Ceramic Society of Japan in 1991, Dr Komeya received an award for his research on nitride ceramics.
3 It can be mentioned that Norton Company, the technically most advanced US manufacturer, chose not to sell its powder in order to protect its proprietary technology.
4 Part of this research was done within the frame of MITI's Fine Ceramics Project. These activities have not resulted in any practically useful patents, but have given an important contribution to the long-term knowledge development in the field of nitride ceramics.
5 The turbocharger rotor was first developed by Nissan and NGK Spark Plug and introduced in 1985. In Japan it is now produced by four companies and commercially used by three auto manufacturers (among which, one, Toyota, has in-house production).
6 Using Wheelwright and Clark's (1992) terminology for classifying development projects based on the degree of change in the product and the manufacturing process, the Nippon Steel case can be designated as an example of a 'platform project'. Toshiba's development of silicon nitride, on the other hand, belongs to the category of 'breakthrough projects'. Such projects involve significant technological change and establish new core products and processes that differ fundamentally from previous generations.

6 CASE ANALYSIS

1 The same cannot be said about consumer goods, where there is no need to establish the same type of activity links and resource ties between manufacturers and users.

2 There may exist a more developed research network among scientists, but this has not been investigated in the study.

3 Membership in an intermarket *keiretsu* can be defined, among other criteria, by a company being represented in the group's presidents' council (*shacho-kai*). Toshiba's president sits on the Mitsui presidents' council, which is called *nimoku-kai*. The concept of *keiretsu* and its importance for understanding the organization of Japanese business is thoroughly discussed in Gerlach (1992b).

4 If a company wants to commercialize a patent, it has to pay a licensing fee to a state-owned body.

5 However, the importance of domestic customers as R&D partners is decreasing for many of the large Swedish companies. It is, among other reasons, the result of the ongoing internationalization of the R&D function (which is partly caused by the large number of foreign acquisitions made in the 1980s).

6 'Tacit' knowledge, to be distinguished from 'explicit' knowledge, is highly personal, hard to formalize, and difficult to communicate. It is deeply rooted in action and in an individual's commitment to a specific context, such as a particular technology, market or company. Tacit knowledge partly consists of technical skills and know-how, partly of mental models, beliefs, and perspectives. In other words, it has an important cognitive dimension which profoundly shapes how different individuals perceive the world around them (Nonaka, 1991, p. 98).

7 See Laage-Hellman (1989, Ch. 4) for a more extensive discussion of technology-related network connections in industrial networks.

8 It can be noted that Nippon Steel also considers its large size to be advantageous when it comes to production. Thanks to its large number of plants it is easier for Nippon Steel than it is for its competitors to keep production for different customers apart.

9 In Axelsson and Håkansson's (1984) terms the purchasing departments of these companies are performing a 'network role'. It means that they are consciously making their purchases so that the supply market structure develops in a direction which is in the long-term interest of the buying firm.

7 A CONCLUDING NOTE ON THE INTERACTING AND NETWORKING BEHAVIOR OF JAPANESE COMPANIES

1 See Gerlach (1992b) for a comprehensive analysis of *keiretsu* and their role in the Japanese economy.

2 A literature survey of Japanese corporate networks and R&D has been made by Harryson (1995).

3 A result of these structural changes in the Japanese subcontracting system is that the number of small and medium-sized manufacturing firms has declined since the mid-1980s (Tselichtchev, 1994, p. 57).

4   In North America the markets may be functioning somewhat differently; that is, the relationships between sellers and buyers tend to be more at arm's length and short term. However, there are reasons to believe that business relationships play a more important role, especially with regard to technological development, than has been attributed to them in the mainstream marketing literature. More recently, it seems that the academic interest in studying buyer–seller relationships has increased in the US.

5   A stable network structure is not necessarily the opposite of rapid technological development. On the contrary, the existence of long-lasting relationships may in fact facilitate the technological exchange in the network and thereby create conditions which favor the development and introduction of new products.

6   For example, in the early 1980s Kyocera started cooperation with Isuzu Motors and some other users. These cooperations resulted in a number of automotive components which are now in production. Asahi Glass tied up with Mitsubishi Motors, and Hitachi Chemicals started development of a ceramic diesel engine together with Nissan Diesel Motor. NGK Spark Plug developed a turbocharger rotor together with Nissan.

7   See, e.g., Takeuchi and Nonaka (1986, pp. 139–40) and Imai *et al.* (1988, pp. 539–42) for a discussion of the use of self-organizing project teams by leading Japanese companies.

8   Based on the literature and widely accepted perceptions of Japanese management it can be questioned if this is typical of Japanese companies. For example, the possibilities to create corporate research laboratories in Japan that are governed by the norms of open inquiry, individually directed research and publication have been questioned by critics arguing that the Japanese companies would have great difficulty in funding the long-term, highly speculative research that is necessary to produce basic knowledge and science-based innovation (Westney, 1991).

9   The case also illustrates the advantage of having a large multi-disciplinary R&D laboratory. This kind of corporate laboratory is common among the big Japanese companies but in many cases has been abolished or downsized by Western companies, for example when decentralizing the R&D function. It can be argued that some Western companies have gone too far in their decentralization of R&D. By moving out the R&D resources to the business divisions the product development becomes more market-oriented, which is good in many ways. At the same time, though, a totally decentralized R&D organization makes it more difficult to achieve cross-fertilization among research groups working in different fields.

10 See Reve (1990) for a discussion about hierarchical and relational control.

11 The concept of tacit knowledge is defined in note 6 of Chapter 6.

Bibliography

Achilladelis, B., Jervis, P. and Robertson, A.B., 1971, *Project SAPPHO: A Study of Success and Failure in Innovation.* Science Policy Research Unit, University of Sussex.

Asanuma, B., 1989, 'Manufacturer–Supplier Relationships in Japan and the Concept of Relation-specific Skill', *Journal of the Japanese and International Economics*, Vol. 3, pp. 1–30.

Automotive Engineering, 1991, 'The Steel and Auto Industries Working Together', Vol. 99, No. 12, pp. 11–17.

Axelsson, B., 1987, 'Supplier Management and Technological Development'. In: Håkansson, H. (ed.), *Industrial Technological Development: A Network Approach.* London: Croom Helm, pp. 128–76.

Axelsson, B. and Easton, G. (eds), 1992, *Industrial Networks: A New View of Reality.* London: Routledge.

Axelsson, B. and Håkansson, H., 1984, *Inköp för konkurrenskraft* (Purchasing for Competitive Power). Stockholm: Liber.

Ballon, R., 1992, *Foreign Competition in Japan: Human Resource Strategies.* London: Routledge.

Basic Facts About Nippon Steel, 1990, Tokyo: Public Relations Dept, Nippon Steel Corporation.

Biemans, V.G., 1992, *Managing Innovations within Networks.* London: Routledge.

Business Week, 1992, 'Learning from Japan', January 27, pp. 38–44.

Campbell, N.C.G., 1991, 'The Borderless Company: Networking in the Japanese Multinational', Paper presented at the 7th IMP Conference in Uppsala, Sweden, September 6–8.

Campbell, N.C.G., Goold, M. and Kase, K., 1990, 'The Role of the Centre in Managing Large Diversified Companies in Japan', *Working Paper*, Manchester Business School.

Dertouzos, M.L., Lester, K.L. and Solow, R.M., 1989, *Made in America.* Cambridge, Mass.: The MIT Press.

Dosi, G., Freeman, C., Nelson, R., Silverberg, G. and Soete, L. (eds), 1988, *Technical Change and Economic Theory.* London: Pinters Publishers.

Enceratec (Product brochure from Engineering Ceramic Technologies, Inc.).

Ford, D. (ed.), 1990, *Understanding Business Markets: Interaction, Relationships and Networks.* London: Academic Press.

Freeman, C., 1982, *The Economics of Industrial Innovation*. London: Frances Pinter.

Gadde, L.-E. and Håkansson, H., 1993, *Professional Purchasing*. London: Routledge.

Gerlach, M.L., 1992a, 'Twilight of the Keiretsu? A Critical Assessment', *Journal of Japanese Studies*, Vol. 18, No. 1, pp. 79–118.

Gerlach, M.L., 1992b, *Alliance Capitalism: The Social Organization of Japanese Business*. Berkeley: University of California Press.

Gerlach, M.L., 1992c, *The Keiretsu: A Primer*. New York: The Japan Society.

Hada, T., 1989, 'Present and Future Trends of Coated Sheet for Automotive Use', Proceedings of The International Conference on Zinc and Zinc Alloy Coated Steel Sheet, Tokyo, The Iron and Steel Institute of Japan.

Håkansson, H., 1982a, *Teknisk utveckling och marknadsföring* (MTC 19) (Technical Development and Marketing). Stockholm: Liber.

Håkansson, H. (ed.), 1982b, *International Marketing and Purchasing of Industrial Goods: An Interaction Approach*. Chichester: John Wiley.

Håkansson, H. (ed.), 1987a, *Industrial Technological Development: A Network Approach*. London: Croom Helm.

Håkansson, H., 1987b, 'Product Development in Networks'. In: Håkansson, H. (ed.), *Industrial Technological Development: A Network Approach*. London: Croom Helm, pp. 84–127.

Håkansson, H., 1989, *Corporate Technological Behaviour: Cooperation and Networks*. London: Routledge.

Håkansson, H., 1990, 'Technological Collaboration in Industrial Networks', *European Management Journal*, Vol. 8, No. 3, pp. 371–9.

Håkansson, H. and Johanson, J., 1993, 'Industrial Functions of Business Relationships'. In: Sharma, D.D. (ed.), *Industrial Networks*, Advances in International Marketing, Vol. 5, Greenwich, Conn.: JAI Press Inc., pp. 13–29.

Håkansson, H. and Snehota, I. (eds), 1995, *Developing Relationships in Business Networks*. London: Routledge.

Håkansson, H., Laage-Hellman, J., Lundgren, A. and Waluszewski, A., 1993, *Teknikutveckling i företaget – ett nätverksperspektiv* (Technological Development in the Company – A Network Perspective). Stockholm: Studentlitteratur.

Hälldahl, L., 1989, 'Materialutveckling i Japan' (Materials Development in Japan), *Utlandsrapport Japan 8905*. Stockholm: Sveriges Tekniska Attachéer.

Harryson, S., 1995, 'Japanese R&D Management: A Holistic Network Approach', Hochschule St Gallen, *Dissertation Nr. 1678*. Bamberg: Difo-Druck GmbH (diss.).

Holden, N.J., 1991, 'Towards an Explanation of Japanese International Networking Behaviour', Paper presented at the 7th IMP Conference in Uppsala, Sweden, September 6–8.

Ichinose, N. (ed.), 1987, *Introduction to Fine Ceramics: Applications in Engineering*. Chichester: John Wiley & Sons.

Imai, K., 1989, 'The Japanese Pattern of Innovation and its Evolution', *Discussion Paper No. 136*, Hitotsubashi University.

Imai, K., Nonaka, I. and Takeuchi, H., 1988, 'Managing the New Product Development Process: How Japanese Companies Learn and Unlearn'. In: Tushman, M.L. and Moore, W.L., *Readings in the Management of Innovation*. Ballinger Publishing Co., pp. 533–61.

Ishiguro, Y., 1991, 'Fine Ceramics Industry Involved in Variety of R&D Projects to Meet Diverse Applications for the Future', *Business Japan*, April, pp. 49–64.

Kimura, H., 1985, 'An Outlook of Fine Ceramics Industry', *Annual Report for Overseas Readers*, Japan Fine Ceramics Association, pp. 14–25.

Kodama, F., 1986, 'Technological Diversification of Japanese Industry', *Science*, Vol. 233, July, pp. 291–6.

Kodama, F., 1992, 'Technology Fusion and the New R&D', *Harvard Business Review*, July–August, pp. 70–8.

Kotler, P., 1988, *Marketing Management. Analysis, Planning Implementation, and Control*. Englewood Cliffs, N.J.: Prentice-Hall.

Laage-Hellman, J., 1984, 'The Role of External Technological Exchange in R&D: An Empirical Study of the Swedish Special Steel Industry', *MTC Research Report No. 18*. Stockholm: Marketing Technology Center.

Laage-Hellman, J., 1987, 'Process Innovation through Technical Cooperation'. In: Håkansson, H. (ed.), *Industrial Technological Development: A Network Approach*. London: Croom Helm, pp. 26–83.

Laage-Hellman, J. 1989, 'Technological Development in Industrial Networks', Acta Univ. Ups., *Comprehensive Summaries of Uppsala Dissertations from the Faculty of Social Sciences 16*, Uppsala (diss.).

Laage-Hellman, J., 1991, 'A Note on the Development of Fine Ceramics in Japan', Institute of Business Research, Hitotsubashi University (mimeo).

Laage-Hellman, J. and Axelsson, B., 1986, 'Bioteknisk FoU i Sverige – forskningsvolym, forskningsinriktning, samarbetsmönster. En studie av det biotekniska FoU-nätverket 1970–85' (Biotechnology R&D in Sweden – Research Volume, Direction of Research, Pattern of Cooperation. A Study of the Biotechnology R&D Network 1970–85), *STU-information 536–1986*. Stockholm: Swedish National Board for Technical Development.

Langrish, J., Gibbons, M., Evans, W.G. and Jevons, F.R., 1972, *Wealth from Knowledge*. London: Macmillan.

Lundgren, A., 1991, *Technological Innovation and Industrial Evolution – The Emergence of Industrial Networks*. Stockholm: The Economic Research Institute, Stockholm School of Economics.

Lundgren, A., 1995, *Technological Innovation and Network Evolution*. London: Routledge.

Lundvall, B.A., 1988, 'Innovation as an Interactive Process: From User–Producer Interaction to the National System of Innovation'. In: Dosi, G. et al. (eds), *Technical Change and Economic Theory*. London: Pinters Publishers, pp. 349–69.

Makino, N., 1992, 'The Advantages of Japan's Management Strategy', *Economic Eye* (Autumn), Vol. 13, No. 3, pp. 18–21.

Malerba, F., 1985, *The Semiconductor Industry. The Economics of Rapid Growth and Decline*. Madison: The University of Wisconsin.

Myers, S. and Marquis, D.G., 1969, *Successful Industrial Innovations*. Washington, DC: National Science Foundation.

Nakatani, I., 1990, 'Effectiveness in Technological Innovation: Keiretsu versus Conglomerates'. In: Heiduk, G. and Yamamura, K. (eds), *Technological Competition and Interdependence. The Search for Policy in the United States, West Germany, and Japan*. Seattle: University of Washington Press, pp. 151–62.

Nonaka, I., 1991, 'The Knowledge-Creating Company', *Harvard Business Review*, November–December, pp. 96–104.

Nonaka, I., 1994, 'A Dynamic Theory of Organizational Knowledge Creation', *Organization Science*, Vol. 5, No. 2, February.

Nonaka, I. and Takeuchi, H., 1995, *The Knowledge-Creating Company*. New York: Oxford University Press.

Reve, T., 1990, 'The Firm as a Nexus of Internal and External Contracts'. In: Aoki, M., Gustafsson, B. and Williamson, O.E. (eds), *The Firm as a Nexus of Treaties*. London: Sage Publications.

Rosenberg, N., 1976, *Perspectives on Technology*. Cambridge: Cambridge University Press.

Rothwell, R., Freeman, C., Horsley, A., Jervis, P., Robertson, A.B. and Townsend, J., 1974, 'SAPPHO Phase II', *Research Policy*, No. 3, pp. 258–91.

Shaw, B., 1991, 'Developing Technological Innovations within Networks', *Entrepreneurship & Regional Development*, 3, pp. 111–28.

Takeuchi, H. and Nonaka, I., 1986, 'The New New Product Development Game', *Harvard Business Review*, January–February, pp. 137–46.

Teramoto, Y., Kanda, M. and Furukawa, K., 1987, 'Network Organization for Inter-Firm Research and Development: Japanese Smaller Firms' Experiences', *Discussion Paper 87–01*, Department of Economics, Meiji Gakuin University.

Toda, M., Kojima, H., Morishita, T., Kanamaru, T. and Arai, K., 1984, 'Development of Two-layered Zn–Fe Alloy Electroplated Steel Sheet – New Coated Steel Sheet for the Automotive Body', International Congress & Exposition, Detroit, Michigan, February 27 to March 2.

Toshiba Today '90, 1990,

Toshiba, *Annual Report*, 1991.

Toshiba Ceramics, *Annual Report*, 1991.

Toshiba Tungaloy, *Annual Report*, 1991.

Tselichtchev, I.S., 1994, 'Rethinking Inter-firm Ties in Japan as a Factor of Competitiveness'. In: Schütte, H., *The Global Competitiveness of the Asian Firm*. London: Macmillan.

Turnbull, P. and Valla, J.-P. (eds), 1986, *Strategies for International Industrial Marketing*. London: Croom Helm.

Van Wolferen, K., 1989, *The Enigma of Japanese Power*, London: Macmillan.

Von Hippel, E., 1988, *The Sources of Innovation*, New York: Oxford University Press.

Waluszewski, A., 1989, 'Framväxten av en ny mekanisk massateknik – en utvecklingshistoria' (The Emergence of a New Mechanical Pulping

Technique – A Development Story), Acta Univ. Ups., *Studia Oeconomiae Negotiorum 31*, Uppsala (diss.).

Westney, D.E., 1991, 'The Evolution of Industrial R&D in Japanese Firms', Paper presented at the Japan in a Global Economy Conference in Stockholm, Sweden, September 5–6.

Wheelwright, S.C. and Clark, K.B., 1992, 'Creating Project Plans to Focus Product Development', *Harvard Business Review*, March–April, pp. 70–82.

Index